ACID REFLUX COOKBOOK

Recipes To Naturally Relieve Heartburn And Manage Acid Reflux In GERD,
Along With A 28-Day Meal Plan For A Healthy Way Of Life.

JENNIFER E. MITCHELL

Table of Contents

Introduction

GRED is a disorder when stomach acid flows back into the tube connecting the mouth and stomach. The esophageal lining may be damaged by acidic backwash. Most individuals will have acid reflux at some time in their life. GERD is described as mild acid reflux occurring twice per week or mild to moderate acid reflux occurring once per week. Asthmatics are more prone to suffer from GERD. As asthma worsens, the lower esophageal sphincter may relax, allowing stomach acid to reflux into the esophagus. Some asthma drugs, such as theophylline, are thought to exacerbate reflux symptoms. In contrast, acid reflux might worsen asthma by making the lungs and airways work harder.

As a result, asthma symptoms may worsen with time. This may induce severe allergies and make the airways considerably more susceptible to smoke and cold air. Most individuals with GERD may manage their symptoms with over-the-counter medications and lifestyle modifications. However, some individuals with GERD may need surgery or harsher medications to alleviate their symptoms. Everyone suffers from gastroesophageal reflux at some time in their life. When you burp, have a sour taste in your mouth, or have heartburn.

Nonetheless, if any of these symptoms make it difficult for you to do daily activities, you should see a physician. Other symptoms of GERD include acid regurgitation (the taste of food after it has been swallowed), difficulty or discomfort swallowing, a persistent sore throat, foul breath, gum inflammation, a persistent or chronic cough, chest pain, laryngitis, or hoarseness, among others. A chest X-ray, an endoscopy to examine the interior of the esophagus, a pH ambulatory acid test to detect the amount of acid in the esophagus, and an esophageal impedance test to evaluate how molecules move in the esophagus may be used to diagnose gastroesophageal reflux disease (GERD). Acid reflux (heartburn) does not infrequently occur for most individuals, but some people experience burning sensations, bloating, and frequent burping after eating. Doctors may identify around 20% of the population with gastroesophageal reflux disease (GERD), a long-term acid reflux illness. The esophageal sphincter shields the esophagus from stomach acid under normal circumstances. This muscular valve allows food to enter the stomach before closing to prevent vomiting. If the sphincter relaxes, food may enter the stomach via the aperture, causing acid reflux.

Diet is the initial step in treating GRED and has a significant role in alleviating acid reflux symptoms. This book is a must-read for everyone who has acid reflux and is concerned that their mild case will develop into a chronic case of GERD, feels constrained in their lifestyle due to this disease, doesn't want to rely on medicine, and wants to live as healthily as possible with acid reflux. It will enable you to avoid taking medication and instead concentrate on consuming foods that can not only treat your acid reflux but also prevent you from contracting this dreadful disease in the first place. This book's primary objective is to assist you in locating meals and meal plans that can improve your health and alleviate your symptoms.

Chapter 1
Managing Acid Reflux through Diet & Lifestyle

By changing your diet, it is possible to control the symptoms of acid reflux. There are several major and minor dietary adjustments; you may make to assist in regulating your symptoms and particular foods to avoid that cause these symptoms. Knowing and adhering to these dietary "rules" for acid reflux may profoundly affect your eating and feeling.

Causes of Heartburn

People call comparable symptoms by several names, including heartburn, acid reflux, indigestion, and GERD. In reality, they are simply variations of the same circumstances. GERD is chronic acid reflux, indigestion, or heartburn that damages the alimentary canal. When acid enters the throat, a condition known as laryngopharyngeal reflux (LPR) occurs.

Occasionally it is caused or aggravated by:

* Smoking
* Certain food & drinks – such as tomatoes, coffee, chocolate, alcohol and fatty/ spicy foods
* Being overweight
* Stress and anxiety
* A rise in some hormones, including progesterone & estrogen
* Pregnancy
* Some medications, such as anti-inflammatory analgesics (like ibuprofen)
* Weakened lower esophageal sphincter
* Increased acid production
* Age
* Bacteria
* Increased intra-abdominal pressure due to overeating, carbonated beverages, obesity, or consuming foods that cause gas.
* A hiatus hernia - when a portion of the stomach protrudes into the chest

Diet & Lifestyle Changes

Changing our way of life requires adjusting determinable factors. It involves aspects that may trigger or exacerbate symptoms, such as dietary modifications or adjustments in daily routine. Although diet does not induce gastroesophageal reflux disease (GERD), meals may increase reflux and its most common symptom, heartburn. Some drugs might exacerbate symptoms. Inform your physician of any drugs you are taking.

Dietary & lifestyle changes often start with what to avoid. These are factors that might cause or exacerbate symptoms.

Examples of foods to limit or avoid from your diet include:

* Caffeine
* High-fat foods
* Chocolate
* Citrus and tomato products
* Peppermint
* Onions
* Alcohol
* Carbonated beverages

Eating well for GERD does not necessitate eliminating all of your favorite meals. Typically, a few easy tweaks to your existing diet are sufficient...

While no scientifically validated GERD diet exists, the following foods might help alleviate or prevent symptoms.

Fruits & Vegetables

Fruits. Choose from a variety of non-citrus fruits, such as bananas, apples, melons, and pears, in place of citrus fruits and juices, such as oranges & lemons.

Vegetables. Choose from the selection of available veggies. Avoid or limit sauces and garnishes that are heavy in fat or irritants, such as tomatoes and onions.

Lean Proteins

Eggs. These are protein-rich. However, if you have a problem with eggs, you should only consume the whites and avoid the higher-fat yolks, which are more likely to induce symptoms.

Lean meat. High-fat meals and fried foods reduce the pressure of the lower esophageal sphincter and delay stomach emptying, raising the risk of acid reflux. Choose grilled, poached, broiled, or baked lean meats.

Complex Carbohydrates

Oatmeal, bread made with whole grains, rice, and couscous. All of them are nutritious sources of complex carbohydrates. Whole grains, including brown rice, provide dietary fiber.

Additionally, various root veggies. These are excellent sources of healthful carbohydrates and digestible fiber, but avoid adding garlic and onions since they are frequent irritants.

Healthier Fats

Fat is a kind of nutrient that is heavy in calories yet essential to a healthy diet. To put it simply, not all fats are the same. Avoid or minimize consumption of saturated fats (often from meat and dairy) and trans fats (in margarine, processed foods and shortenings). Replace them with unsaturated fats from vegetables or seafood in moderation. Here are several examples:

Unsaturated fatty acids Oils such as sesame, canola, olive, avocados, sunflower, peanuts & peanut butter, and other nuts & seeds are examples.

Unsaturated fatty acids include safflower, flaxseed, soybean, maize, walnut oils, soybeans, tofu, salmon, and trout.

Not everyone experiences heartburn for the same reasons. While one person's trigger may be a huge meal and spicy food, another's may be late-night exercise or laying down after eating. You may make a food journal to document your food, drink, activity, time, and any subsequent symptoms. Another advantage of keeping a meal diary is the possibility of establishing a link between any atypical or unrelated heartburn triggers, such as high blood pressure, depression, anxiety, or other conditions. After keeping a dietary journal for weeks, you should discuss the findings with your physician.

You and your doctor will be able to determine the pattern of your acid reflux & heartburn, as well as identify heartburn triggers if you keep a food diary. Most significantly, it will assist your physician in diagnosing GERD and initiating therapy.

There are a variety of activities you might be carrying out that contribute to heartburn, as well as steps you may do to avoid it.

Position

Gravity has a crucial function in regulating reflux. For those with a less-than-perfect lower esophageal sphincter (LES), lying down after a heavy meal causes reflux and heartburn. Consider if your heartburn happens after meals, at night, or when you sleep if you feel it. Maintaining an upright position until digestion is complete might avoid heartburn. Consider elevating the head of your bed or integrating a triangular wedge to position your esophagus above your stomach if nighttime heartburn happens often. Using an additional pillow or two may also avoid reflux. Avoid exercise after a meal. It drives food past a weaker sphincter by contracting the abdominal muscles. This is particularly true for chores requiring bending, like lifting or floor cleaning. Do not lie down within three hours after eating. This is when acid production is strongest, so eat supper early and avoid eating before bed. Multiple studies have shown that sleeping on the left side seems to be the optimal posture for GERD sufferers. Sleeping on the left side minimizes reflux episodes and esophageal exposure to stomach acid. Other sleeping positions, especially the back, might increase the likelihood of reflux.

How you eat

How you eat is likely more considerable than what you consume. A heavy meal will cause the stomach to empty slowly and put more pressure on LES. A night snack is ideal for preventing acid reflux while lying down. Eating early in the evening is preferable, so digestion is complete before sleep. You may try eating your major meal at lunch and a smaller meal for supper. All meals must be consumed in a calm, stress-free environment. During and for some hours following a meal, going to the kitchen to get food and executing other chores, such as watching children, should be prohibited. Smaller meals and a relaxed, upright posture should help reduce acid reflux.

Consume smaller, more regular meals than a few substantial ones throughout the day. This facilitates digestion and may avoid heartburn.

What you eat

Certain meals impair the sphincter's capacity to prevent reflux and should be avoided before laying down or engaging in physical activity. These vary from one to another. Many individuals find fats, onions, & chocolate to be especially problematic. Alcohol often causes heartburn by weakening the lower esophageal sphincter (LES), irritating the esophagus, and boosting stomach acid production. Coffee (both caffeinated & decaffeinated), cola, tomato juice, tea, and citrus juice might exacerbate symptoms by stimulating the esophagus or promoting stomach acid production. Additional meals may irritate certain individuals; avoiding or reducing them for some time may be beneficial upon their detection.

Some oral drugs, including potassium supplements and the antibiotic tetracycline, may burn if allowed to remain in the esophagus for an extended period. Always consume the medicine upright and with a large amount of water to ensure safety.

Other factors

The nicotine found in cigarettes might cause the lower esophageal sphincter to become weakened and increases stomach acid production. This muscle regulates the entrance between the esophagus and stomach. When it is closed, it prevents stomach acid and other contents from coming back up.

Wear loose-fitting clothing to alleviate stomach strain, which may aggravate heartburn and reflux.

Do not consume gum or hard sweets. Swallowing air with gum and hard candies might result in belching and reflux.

Being obese might cause acid reflux. Excess abdominal fat exerts pressure on the abdomen, and even a minor weight reduction improves many individuals' well-being. Heartburn is common during pregnancy, especially during the first 3 months. Certain hormones weaken the lower esophageal sphincter (LES), and an expanding belly promotes reflux. Generally, if a woman has not gained excessive weight, her heartburn resolves after delivery. Stress and intense emotions may also contribute to heartburn.

Antacids may alleviate heartburn momentarily by neutralizing gastric acid. Other over-the-counter medications that lower acid production may be available for occasional and short-term heartburn treatment.

You should visit your primary care physician if heartburn develops more than two per week with the preceding remedies.

Chapter 2
Ways to Reduce Anxiety with New Healthy Habits

Anxiety is the body's natural reaction to stress. Contrarily, having anxiety may be stressful in and of itself, which can start a vicious cycle. Anxiety and acid reflux may be closely related. According to some studies, anxiety and stress may worsen acid reflux symptoms.

The authors of the research provide several physical explanations for this.

- The lower esophageal sphincter, a muscular band that seals off the stomach and prevents acid from seeping into the esophagus, may become less constricted due to anxiety.
- Muscle tightness that lasts for a long time might be brought on by anxiety and stress. If the stomach's surrounding muscles are impacted, the pressure within the organ may rise, and the acid may rise.
- High levels of anxiety may lead to more stomach acid being produced.

Numerous individuals sometimes have acid reflux and occasionally experience anxiety when exposed to stressful situations. Addressing or avoiding symptoms when one or both appear often is critical. Additionally, because the signs of anxiety & acid reflux may exacerbate one another, managing the situation may help overcome this vicious cycle.

Lifestyle modifications are simple but effective treatments for depression and anxiety and are crucial to a comprehensive healing plan. It becomes sensible to start with lifestyle modifications immediately since they may sometimes relieve sadness or anxiety. However, you should also seek immediate professional assistance if you are experiencing moderate to severe anxiety. Likewise, get professional assistance if your minor depressive symptoms don't improve in a few months.

The following are changes to one's way of life that may be helpful.

Exercise

The most crucial first step is exercise. Exercise is useful in improving mood and lowering depressive symptoms in several well-designed research. Regarding anxiety, several studies have shown that participating in more physical exercise, particularly mindful movement practices like yoga, tai chi, and qigong, improve anxiety symptoms and digestive issues.

Exercise increases the body's serotonin and endorphins, two neurotransmitters that lessen sadness. Exercise routine increases your self-esteem, increase self-assurance, fosters a feeling of empowerment and strengthens relationships and social ties

Diet

One of the body's most metabolically active organs, the brain, requires a constant supply of nutrients to operate. Poor diets may lack the nutrients to make neurotransmitters, leading to anxiety or depressive symptoms.

- Maintain a healthy diet. To comply with current dietary recommendations, fill your platter with fresh, whole foods, drink enough water, obtain adequate calcium, and limit your intake of trans fats.
- Mind your intestinal health. A healthy digestive tract may be supported by taking supplementary probiotics that include two or even more live cultures (such as lactobacillus or Bifidobacterium) and consuming fermented foods like yoghurt and miso.
- Cut the sugary drinks. Fruit punch, soda, and sweetened tea may exacerbate sadness. According to recent research, those who consume more than four cups/cans of soda daily have a 30% higher risk of developing depression than those who do not.
- Switch to decaf. Decaffeinated coffee could be the best option for certain people since some research indicates that long-term caffeine intake has been connected with anxiety. If you regularly use caffeine, reducing your intake gradually will be most tolerable.

Alcohol

Alcohol increases stomach acid production and esophageal sensitivity, which increases the likelihood of experiencing heartburn. Alcohol relaxes the lower esophageal sphincter, releasing stomach acid into the esophagus. Even though alcohol is a depressant, people that are depressed have greater issues with alcohol usage. People may use alcohol as a kind of "self-medication" to dull the discomfort of their despair.

Those who are depressed need to give up drinking. If alcohol misuse is the root cause of depression, it must be treated immediately.

Sleep

The lower esophageal sphincter (LES), a valve that separates the stomach from the esophagus, might malfunction due to lack of sleep and exhaustion, enabling stomach acid to pass up into an esophagus. GERD and acid reflux might result from this LES dysfunction.

Because sleep replenishes the neurotransmitters necessary to promote mood, poor sleep significantly impacts mood. So, to keep our brains in equilibrium and combat sadness and anxiety, we need restorative sleep.

Major depression is more likely to strike individuals who don't get enough sleep each night, either in quantity or quality. Additionally, it has been shown that sleep-deprived individuals have a significantly larger propensity to label neutral sights as "negative," making even commonplace objects appear more dangerous and provoking anxiety. Make getting the necessary quantity of restful sleep a top priority.

Thoughts and Emotions

In addition to disrupting the body's hormonal balance and depleting the brain chemicals necessary for sensations of happiness and calm, negative attitudes and helpless and hopeless sentiments may also negatively affect our immune system or other bodily systems.

Certain mental exercises, like positive thinking or meditation, may alter how we see the environment and help us feel more at ease, resilient, and content. Other studies have also discovered numerous positive attitudes that might lessen melancholy and anxiety, including those that emphasize forgiveness, appreciation, and compassion. These may be acquired via training.

Stress Reduction

Depression and anxiety are exacerbated by excessive stress. Despite the face of stress, developing coping mechanisms to lessen the negative effects of stress may help one feel in control and at ease.

Three strategies for reducing stress

- Determine what stresses you out and consider making adjustments in your life to lessen these pressures.
- Learn relaxing strategies to lessen your sensitivity to stimuli and develop thoughtful, constructive reactions.
- Develop resilience to cope as best you can with unavoidable stresses in life.

Social Support

Strong connections and social networks lessen loneliness and isolation, two major risk factors for anxiety. Seeking out friends and family may help us cope with anxiety by supporting and assisting us in making realistic assessments of risks, yet anxiety can sometimes lead us to avoid other people and become isolated.

Purpose

According to extensive studies, those with a significant sense of purpose are more prepared for life's ups and downs. A person with a strong sense of purpose can withstand challenges psychologically and still feel content with their life, even when they are having a challenging day. According to research, such long-term resilience may eventually result in less anxiety and more enjoyment. Spirituality also enables individuals to persist and overcome obstacles. Strong spiritual convictions may enable you to find purpose in challenging situations.

Heartburn may be brought on by anxiety in several ways, including muscular tension, changes in digestion, and hormonal changes. It may also be an anxiety trigger, particularly for those who are hypersensitive as a consequence of panic episodes or health anxieties. Although anxiety must also be handled to prevent symptoms, heartburn is often treated with dietary modifications and over-the-counter drugs.

Chapter 3
Foods to eat and Foods to Avoid

Acid reflux (heartburn) is common, and most people experience it at least sometimes. However, for some individuals, it occurs practically every time they eat, causing painful burning, bloating, and belching. Gastroesophageal reflux disease (GERD) affects around 20% of the population.

A person's diet is the first line of treatment for gastroesophageal reflux disease (GERD) because of its powerful effect on reducing acid reflux symptoms.

Foods that could give you heartburn

Foods often identified as heartburn triggers might lengthen the time food remains in the stomach by relaxing the esophageal sphincter and delaying digestion. Foods with a lot of fat, salt, or spice, like:

* Fast food
* Chilli powder & pepper (black, white, cayenne)
* Fried food
* Pizza
* Potato chips & other processed snacks
* Cheese
* Fatty meats, such as sausage and bacon

Other foods that may contribute to the issue include:

* Citrus fruits, i.e. grapefruit, lemons, orange, lime and tangerine
* Tomato-based sauces
* Whole & 2% milk, whole milk yogurt & cheeses
* Full-fat sour cream
* Butter & margarine (only small amounts recommended)
* Sauces & dips
* Chocolate & high-fat dessert
* Bologna
* Chocolate milk & hot chocolate
* Ice-cream
* Garlic

- Fried and creamed vegetables
- Onions
- Caffeinated & Carbonated beverages
- Peppermint
- Alcohol

Moderation is important because many people don't want to give up all of these foods.

Foods that reduce the risk of acid reflux

You may consume a variety of foods to help avoid acid reflux. Foods to eat:

- Fennel
- Ginger
- Brown Rice
- Non-citrus fruits
- low-fat yoghurt
- Low-fat cheeses
- Skim / 1% milk
- Low-fat meats
- low-fat cookies & cakes
- Skinless poultry
- Mild Green Vegetables (green beans, celery, lettuce, sweet peppers, etc.)
- Lean meats & seafood
- Egg whites; (limit yolks as of fat content)
- Healthy fats (avocado, flaxseed, olive oil etc.)

Stock up on these three types of food in your kitchen:

High-fiber foods

Fibrous meals help you feel full, which lowers your risk of overeating, which may worsen heartburn. Here are some high-fiber foods:

- Couscous, oatmeal, & brown rice are good examples of whole grains.
- Sweet potatoes, beets, & carrots are root vegetables.
- Green foods, including broccoli, green beans & asparagus.

Alkaline foods

Foods are pH-scale-dependent in some way (indicates acid levels). Low-pH foods are acidic and much more likely to induce reflux than those with a higher ph. Higher pH values are alkaline and may help counteract very acidic stomach contents.

ACIDIC	ALKALINE
3 pH: club soda, carbonated water, Energy drinks, vinegar, goat cheese, processed food, lamb	**7 pH:** butter, margarine, tap water, unsalted fresh raw milk, and oil, except olive oil.
4 pH: Popcorn, buttermilk, cream cheese, prunes pastries, cheese, pasta, pork, wine, black tea, beer, pickles, roasted nuts, chocolates, vinegar, beef, tomato sauce, blackberries, cranberries,	**8 pH:** almonds, apples, tomatoes, olive, grapefruits, corn, mushrooms, soybeans, turnip, bell pepper, peaches, radish, cherries, wild rice, pineapple, peaches apricot, strawberries, bananas,
5 pH: Most purified water, coffee, distilled water, sweetened fruit juices, white bread, pistachios, peanuts, wheat, molasses, nuts, sugar, potatoes, butter, rhubarb, chicken/ turkey, black beans, lentils, molasses, white rice wheat bran,	**9 pH:** green tea, lettuce, peas, eggplant, sweet potatoes, green beans, blueberries, Avocadoes, beets, figs, pears, grapes, melons, kiwi, mangoes, tangerines, dates, mangoes, papayas, celery, olive oil,
6 pH: eggs, fruit juices, grain, fish, cooked beans, tea, cooked spinach, coconut, soy milk, lima beans, brown rice, plums, barley, oats, cocoa, liver, oyster, milk yogurt, salmon, tuna	**10 pH:** artichoke, broccoli, cabbage, Brussel sprouts, spinach, cauliflower, cucumber, carrots, lemons, seaweed, limes, asparagus, radish, kale, onions, collard greens,

Alkaline foods good for GERD are:

- Melons
- Bananas
- Cauliflower
- Nuts
- Fennel

Watery foods

Consuming meals high in water might weaken and dilute gastric acid. Select foods like:

- Cucumber
- Celery
- Herbal tea
- Lettuce
- Broth-based soups
- Watermelon

Home Remedies for Heartburn

Some meals may provide symptom alleviation. Try the following, possibly:

Milk

Milk is often recommended as a heartburn remedy. But you must remember that there are several types of milk, including whole milk with all the fat, 2% fat, or skim and nonfat milk. Milk fat might make acid reflux symptoms worse.

However, nonfat milk may temporarily obstruct the stomach lining from the stomach's acidic contents and relieve heartburn symptoms right away. The same calming effects are present in low-fat yoghurt, which contains plenty of probiotics. Good bacteria enhance digestion.

Ginger

The therapeutic benefits of ginger make it one of the greatest digestive aids. Its natural alkalinity & anti-inflammatory properties decrease inflammation in the digestive tract. If you feel heartburn, try some ginger tea.

Apple cider vinegar

Although there isn't sufficient evidence to support it, many believe apple cider vinegar relieves acid reflux. However, since it contains a strong acid that could irritate the esophagus, you shouldn't ever consume it when fully focused. Instead, mix a little bit with warm water and consume it with meals.

Lemon water

While a small amount of lemon juice combined with warm water & honey has had an alkalizing effect balancing stomach acid, lemon juice is often considered quite acidic. Additionally, honey contains organic antioxidants that protect cells' health.

Treatment for GERD often involves a mix of medication and lifestyle modifications. However, if reflux symptoms are chronic, a gastroenterologist should be seen for a complete assessment so they can determine the underlying reason and go through the range of potential treatments.

Shopping List for acid reflux

* Vegetables: Try to get as many leafy greens & root vegetables such as (beets, sweet potatoes & carrots.), and cruciferous vegetables such as (cauliflower & broccoli).
* Fruits: Try to get fruits like Bananas, apricots, pears, apples, honeydew melon, plums & coconut.
* Grains: Try to get whole grains such as quinoa, rolled oats, bulgur & amaranth.
* Protein: choose lean protein that is skinless, like skinless chicken breasts & 90 % lean ground turkey. Also get fish, pork, tofu, & beans.

Chapter 4
Breakfast Recipes

Note: If you find any ingredients that trigger your acid reflux, feel free to omit or change that ingredient.

1. California Scrambled Eggs and Avocado

Preparation Time: 8 minutes

Total Time: 10 minutes

Servings: 1

Difficulty Level: Easy

Nutritional Information
Calories: 313 Kcal, Protein: 14 g, Carbohydrates: 8 g, Fat: 25 g, Fiber: 4 g

---

INGREDIENTS

* 2 Large Brown Grade A, Free-Range Organic Eggs
* 1 tsp of extra-virgin olive oil
* 1 pinch of sea salt
* 2 tsp of fresh cilantro
* 1/8 tsp of Sea Salt, Mediterranean, Coarse
* 1/2 whole Avocado

INSTRUCTIONS

This recipe is for 1 serving only.

Heat the oil over medium heat in a medium nonstick skillet without PFOA. Whisk the eggs, cilantro, and 1/8 teaspoon salt in a liquid measuring cup until well blended. Pour this egg mixture into a skillet & gently scramble it for approximately 1 minute plus 15 seconds or until it is no longer runny. Add the avocado and the last sprinkle of salt before placing it in a dish or bowl.

2. Sweet Potato Protein Hash

Preparation Time: 45 minutes

Total Time: 1 hour 30 minutes

Servings: 4

Difficulty Level: Medium

Nutritional Information
Calories: 342 Kcal, Protein: 13 g, Carbohydrates: 23 g, Fat: 22 g, Fiber: 7 g

INGREDIENTS

- 2 cooked medium sweet potato
- 1/2 tsp of Sea Salt
- 2 Avocados fruit without skin & seed, raw, California
- 1 tbsp of olive oil
- 8 oz of Extra Firm Tofu
- 3 tbsp of Hemp Seed

INSTRUCTIONS

This recipe is for 4 servings only. Leftovers can be stored in an airtight container in the fridge for 1-2 days.

Set the oven to 350 degrees F. Sweet potatoes, spices, & olive oil are combined in a bowl. Potatoes should be well covered after mixing. Bake for 40 minutes, or until soft, on a cookie sheet.

Olive oil is drizzled in a pan over medium heat. Then, add the tofu, constantly stirring to prevent scorching. Tofu will break apart. Stir the cooked sweet potato into the mixture after adding it to the pan. On a platter, spread the tofu/potato mixture and garnish with avocado slices & hemp seeds.

3. Beet & Berries Smoothie Bowl

Preparation Time: 10 minutes

Total Time: 10 minutes

Servings: 2

Difficulty Level: Easy

Nutritional Information
Calories: 195 Kcal, Protein: 18 g, Carbohydrates: 24 g, Fat: 3 g, Fiber: 7 g

---

INGREDIENTS

* Four ice cubes
* 1 cup peeled and chopped beets.
* ¼ cup of fresh cranberries
* 1 cup of fresh strawberries
* 1 cup of almond milk: unsweetened
* Vanilla protein powder: 1 scoop

INSTRUCTIONS

This recipe is for 2 servings only.

In a high-powered blender, combine all ingredients and process until smooth. Transfer the smoothie to a serving bowl and finish with your preferred toppings. Serve and enjoy it.

4. Oatmeal Yogurt Bowl

Preparation Time: 10 minutes

Total Time: 10 minutes

Servings: 2

Difficulty Level: Easy

Nutritional Information
Calories: 255 Kcal, Protein: 10 g, Carbohydrates: 47 g, Fat: 3 g, Fiber: 6 g

INGREDIENTS

- 1 cup old-fashioned oats
- 2 cups of water
- ½ cup of fresh strawberries
- 6 ounces Greek yogurt (non-fat plain)

INSTRUCTIONS

This recipe is for 2 servings only.

Bring water to a boil in a saucepan over medium heat. Add oats and cook, stirring periodically, for around 5 minutes. Switch off the heat and pour the yoghurt into the oats. Uniformly distribute the oatmeal into serving cups. Serve with strawberry slices on top of each mug.

5. Zucchini Bread

Preparation Time: 10 minutes

Total Time: 1 hr. 20 minutes

Servings: 8

Difficulty Level: Medium

Nutritional Information
Calories: 285 kcal, Protein: 7 g, Carbohydrates: 44 g, Fat: 9 g, Fibers: 5 g

---

INGREDIENTS

- 1/2 cup of unsweetened applesauce
- 1/4 cup of canola oil
- 6 egg whites
- 2 teaspoons of vanilla extract
- 1/2 cup of sugar
- 1 1/4 cups of all-purpose flour; (plain)
- 1 teaspoon of baking powder
- 1 1/4 cups of whole-wheat flour; (whole-meal)
- 3 teaspoons of ground cinnamon
- 1 teaspoon of baking soda
- 2 cups of shredded zucchini
- 1 1/2 cups of unsweetened crushed pineapple
- 1/2 cup of chopped walnuts

INSTRUCTIONS

This recipe is for 18 servings only. Leftover can be stored in an airtight container in the fridge for 4 days.

Preheat the oven to 350 degrees Fahrenheit. Spray two loaf pans of 9-by-5-inch lightly with cooking spray.

Combine the canola oil, egg whites, sugar, applesauce, and vanilla in a large mixing bowl. Beat the mixture with an electric mixer on low speed until thick and bubbly.

Add baking soda, powder, and cinnamon to a small flour bowl. Combine the flour in a small mixing bowl. Set aside 1/2 cup.

Combine egg white mixture with flour and beat on medium speed with an electric mixer until thoroughly combined. Stir in the walnuts, zucchini, and pineapple until everything is well-mixed. Use the remaining 1/2 cup of flour, and adjust the batter's consistency by adding 1 tablespoon at a time. The batter must be thick and not runny.

Half of the batter should be poured into the prepared pan. Bake for 50 minutes or until a tester inserted in the middle of the loaves comes out clean. Allow 10 minutes for the bread to cool in the pans on a wire rack. Remove the loaves from the pans and place them on a cooling rack to cool fully. Serve each loaf cut into nine 1-inch pieces.

6. Avocado & Berry Breakfast Bowls

Preparation Time: 6 minutes

Total Time: 6 minutes

Servings: 2-3

Difficulty Level: Easy

Nutritional Information
Calories: 163 Kcal, Protein: 12 g, Carbohydrates: 13 g, Fat: 7 g, Fiber: 5 g

---

INGREDIENTS

- 1/2 avocado peeled and diced.
- 1/2 cup frozen raspberries
- 1/2 cup low-fat Greek yogurt

INSTRUCTIONS

This recipe is for 2-3 servings only.

In a high-powered processor, combine all of the ingredients. Blend until entirely smooth. Enjoy in chilled serving cups or sundae glasses.

7. Puréed Banana Oats

Preparation Time: 10 minutes

Total Time: 15 minutes

Servings: 2

Difficulty Level: Easy

Nutritional Information
Calories: 129 Kcal, Protein: 4 g, Carbohydrates: 27 g, Fat: 1 g, Fiber: 3 g

---

INGREDIENTS

- 1 banana
- 1/4 cup ground oats
- 8 oz. boiling water

INSTRUCTIONS

This recipe is for 2 servings only.

Peel and cut the banana into slices. Steam bananas for 10 minutes. Mix boiling water and oatmeal in a separate bowl. Blend oatmeal and banana until you have a smooth consistency. You may add more water or oatmeal, depending on your preferred consistency. Serve warm.

8. Chicken & Zucchini Pancakes

Preparation Time: 10 minutes

Total Time: 30 minutes

Servings: 2

Difficulty Level: Medium

Nutritional Information
Calories: 180 Kcal, Protein: 7 g, Carbohydrates: 11 g, Fat: 12 g, Fiber: 4 g

---

INGREDIENTS

- Salt to taste
- 2 cups of shredded zucchinis
- 1 tablespoon of olive oil (extra-virgin)
- ¼ cup of cooked shredded chicken
- 1 beaten egg
- ¼ cup of finely chopped scallion
- ¼ cup of coconut flour

INSTRUCTIONS

Place zucchini in a colander and season with salt. Let it set for 8-10 minutes. Squeeze the zucchini thoroughly and place them in a mixing bowl. Blend the squeezed zucchini with the remaining ingredients and stir well. Heat the oil in a wide nonstick skillet over medium heat. Place 1/4 cup of the zucchini mixture in a preheated skillet and spread evenly. Cook for 3-4 minutes on each side. Continue for the rest of the mixture. Serve warm.

9. Pumpkin Overnight Oats

Preparation Time: 10 minutes

Total Time: 10 minutes

Servings: 2

Difficulty Level: Medium

Nutritional Information
Calories: 224 kcal, Protein: 6 g, Carbohydrates: 41 g, Fat: 4 g, Fiber: 6 g

---

INGREDIENTS

- 3 tablespoons of pumpkin puree
- ⅓ cup of unsweetened almond milk; (other non-dairy milk)
- ½ teaspoon of vanilla extract
- 2 teaspoons of pure maple syrup
- ½ cup of rolled oats
- ¼ teaspoon of ground cinnamon
- Toasted pumpkin seeds/pecans for garnish
- Pinch of salt

INSTRUCTIONS

This recipe is for 2 servings only.

In a pint-size jar, combine the milk, oats, pumpkin, vanilla, cinnamon, maple syrup, and salt; mix well. Refrigerate overnight, covered. If desired, garnish with pumpkin seeds (or nuts) before serving.

10. Chia Pudding

Preparation Time: 15 minutes

Total Time: 45 minutes

Servings: 4

Difficulty Level: Easy

Nutritional Information
Calories: 187 Kcal, Protein: 9 g, Carbohydrates: 11 g, Fat: 12 g, Fiber: 8 g

---

INGREDIENTS

- 4 oz Soft Tofu
- 1 cup of blueberries
- 1 ½ cups unsweetened Almond Milk;
- 1/4 cup of Sliced Almonds
- 1/2 tsp of Pure Almond Extract
- 1/4 cup of Chia Seeds

INSTRUCTIONS

This recipe is for 4 servings only.

Combine tofu, almond milk, and extract in a blender (or food processor). Blend until the mixture is smooth and thoroughly blended. Transfer to a bowl, mix in the chia seeds and set aside for 10 minutes. Heat a small pan over low-medium heat, add the almond slices, and constantly stir until they are gently toasted. Remove the pan from the heat and put it aside. Add blueberries to the chia seed mixture gently. Chia pudding should be refrigerated before serving. Distribute equally among four small dishes; if preferred, top with the toasted almonds and more blueberries.

11. French Toast

Preparation Time: 10 minutes

Total Time: 45 minutes

Servings: 2

Difficulty Level: Easy

Nutritional Information
Calories: 194 kcal, Protein: 10 g, Carbohydrates: 16g, Fat: 10g, Fiber: 2g

---

INGREDIENTS

- 3 tbsp. low fat butter
- 1 tsp. brown sugar
- ¼ tsp. ground nutmeg
- 2 tbsp. pure maple syrup
- 2 large eggs
- 4 slices of sourdough bread
- 1/2 tsp. of vanilla extract
- 6 tbsp. skim milk

INSTRUCTIONS

This recipe is for 2 servings only.

Mix the eggs, vanilla, milk, nutmeg and brown sugar until well mixed. Pour the paste over the bread and soak the bread entirely. Soak it for a few minutes and cook on the heated greased skillet for 5 minutes. Cook on both sides. Serve it warm with maple syrup.

12. Zucchini Fritters

Preparation Time: 5 minutes

Total Time: 30 minutes

Servings: 2

Difficulty Level: Easy

Nutritional Information
Calories:186 kcal, Protein: 12g, Carbohydrates: 21g, Fat: 6g, Fibers: 3g

INGREDIENTS

- 1/4 cup raw quick oats
- 3 large eggs
- extra-virgin olive oil as needed for cooking.
- 1/2 small zucchini (grated)

INSTRUCTIONS

This recipe is for 2 servings only. Leftovers can be stored in an airtight container in the fridge for 1-2 days.

Whisk the oats, eggs, and zucchini in a mixing bowl until well combined. Spray or brush a non-stick pan with a thin layer of oil, then spoon the batter into the pan. Keep an eye on the heat on these. You may need to reduce the heat to medium and cook these for a little longer. Cook the eggs entirely without burning them. Make the required adjustments. When the fritters are done, remove them from the pan and serve with a dollop of hummus.

13. Panzanella Breakfast Salad

Preparation Time: 10 minutes

Total Time: 30 minutes

Servings: 4

Difficulty Level: Easy

Nutritional Information
Calories: 247 kcal, Protein: 12 g, Carbohydrates: 34 g, Fat: 7 g, Fibers: 9 g

---

INGREDIENTS

- 2 medium cucumbers
- 4 medium Sweet Potatoes
- 1/4 tsp of sea salt
- 2 tbsp of extra-virgin olive oil
- 4 cups of Kale, Raw
- 4 slices of 7 Grain Sourdough, Whole Wheat Bread
- 4 Eggs, Large, Pasture-Raised Organic, Grade-A
- ½ cup Basil leaves
- 1/8 tsp of Sea Salt

INSTRUCTIONS

This recipe is for 4 servings only.

Turn the oven on to 450 degrees F. On a baking pan, arrange the sweet potatoes. Apply olive oil, then season with salt. For 20 mins, roast them, with a half turn. While the potatoes are roasting, slice the cucumber and mix it with kale, basil oil and salt, then give it a 3–5-minute gentle hand massage. Slice your bread into bite-sized chunks after lightly toasting. Toss the bread, vegetables and roasted potatoes together gently. Poach an egg and place one on top of each of the four portions.

14. Kale and Sweet Potato Baked Frittata Cups

Preparation Time: 15 minutes

Total Time: 40 minutes

Servings: 4

Difficulty Level: Easy

Nutritional Information
Calories: 257 kcal, Protein: 16 g, Carbohydrates: 19 g, Fat: 13 g, Fibers: 3 g

INGREDIENTS

- 6 Free Range, Large Eggs
- 1 second spray of Organic Olive Oil
- 1 tbsp of Olive Oil; Extra Virgin
- 1/2 tsp of Sea Salt
- 3 sweet potato; raw sweet potato
- 1 1/2 oz of Baby Kale
- 2 tbsp of Basil, fresh
- 1/2 cup of low-fat mozzarella Cheese

INSTRUCTIONS

This recipe is for 4 servings only.

Set the oven to 375 degrees F. Apply cooking spray to the eight cups of a nonstick muffin pan. The eggs & salt should be beaten together in a big bowl. Place aside. Heat the oil over medium-high heat in a medium- or large stick-resistant skillet. Sauté the sweet potato for approximately 5-10 minutes or until they start to brown. Add kale, cook, until completely wilted, and turn off the heat. Stir immediately after adding the sweet potato-kale blend to the egg mixture. Stir in the cheese & Basil until evenly distributed. Pour equally the egg mixture into each muffin cup. About 18 minutes into baking, all egg frittata cups should be just set. Take out of the muffin tin and serve hot.

15. Oatmeal Breakfast Cookies

Preparation Time: 10 minutes

Total Time: 25 minutes

Servings: 6

Difficulty Level: Medium

Nutritional Information
Calories: 256 kcal, Protein: 10 g, Carbohydrates: 31 g, Fat: 10 g, Fibers: 5 g

---

INGREDIENTS

- 2 cups quick oats
- 1 teaspoon ground cinnamon
- 1/2 cup creamy unsalted nut butter of choice
- ½ cup chopped walnuts
- 3 tablespoons ground flaxseed
- 1/3 cup unsweetened dried cranberries
- ¼ cup pumpkin puree
- ¼ cup maple syrup
- ½ teaspoon salt

INSTRUCTIONS

This recipe is for 6 servings only. Leftovers can be stored in an airtight container for 4-5 days.

Put the oven on to a temperature of 325 degrees Fahrenheit. Put to the side a large baking sheet that has been prepared for baking by lining it with either parchment paper or a silicone baking mat. Mix the oats, nut butter, walnuts, cranberries, pumpkin puree, maple syrup, flaxseed, cinnamon, and salt in a large mixing bowl, until a dough ball forms. Pack the dough into the scoop as tightly as possible using a large scoop designed for ice cream. Spread the batter out evenly on the baking sheet that has been prepared. Even though the cookies won't spread while baking, you still need to ensure they are evenly distributed around the baking sheet. Bake the cookies for 15-20 minutes until they are golden brown. Take the pan out of the oven and set it somewhere else to cool down completely.

Chapter 5
Smoothies

Note: If you find any ingredients that trigger your acid reflux, feel free to omit or change that ingredient.

16. Banana-Apple Smoothie

Preparation Time: 5 minutes

Total Time: 5 minutes

Servings: 2

Difficulty Level: Easy

Nutritional Information
Calories: 179 kcal, Protein: 8 g, Carbohydrates: 31 g, Fat: 3 g, Fiber: 3 g

---

INGREDIENTS

- 2 tbsp of oat bran
- 1/2 banana peeled: chunks.
- 1/4 cup of skim milk
- 1/2 cup of plain yogurt
- 1 tbsp honey
- 1/2 cup applesauce: unsweetened

INSTRUCTIONS

This recipe is for 2 servings only.

Add yogurt, banana, applesauce, honey, and milk to a blender and blend to a smooth texture. Then add oat bran and keep blending until thickened.

17. Acid Reflux Smoothie

Preparation Time: 5 minutes

Total Time: 5 minutes

Servings: 2

Difficulty Level: Easy

Nutritional Information
Calories: 231 kcal, Protein: 9 g, Carbohydrates: 32 g, Fat: 7 g, Fiber: 7 g

---

INGREDIENTS

- 5 fresh basil; leaves
- ¾ cup OF cashew milk
- ½ inch of ginger root
- ¼ cup of spinach
- 1 banana frozen
- ⅓ cup of rolled oats
- ½ pear

INSTRUCTIONS

This recipe is for 2 servings only.

Spinach, basil leaves, & cashew milk should all be well blended. Blend again after adding the remaining ingredients. For a chilled, refreshing smoothie, serve over ice.

18. Alkaline Smoothie

Preparation Time: 3 minutes

Total Time: 5 minutes

Servings: 2

Difficulty Level: Easy

Nutritional Information
Calories: 122 kcal, Protein: 5 g, Carbohydrates: 16 g, Fat: 4 g, Fiber: 4 g

INGREDIENTS

- 1 cup of watermelon cubed
- 1 cup of almond milk
- 1/2 small banana
- 5 strawberries frozen
- 1 handful of fresh spinach
- 1 cup of ice
- 1 teaspoon of chia seeds

INSTRUCTIONS

This recipe is for 2 servings only.

Add the ingredients to the blender. Blend the greens with chia seeds, half the ice, the banana, and half the almond milk to avoid a dark smoothie. Then add watermelon with ice and milk. Enjoy the smoothies after pouring them into the same glass.

19. Blueberry-Pineapple Smoothie

Preparation Time: 5 minutes

Total Time: 5 minutes

Servings: 2

Difficulty Level: Easy

Nutritional Information
Calories: 80 kcal, Protein: 2 g, Carbohydrates: 18 g, Fat: 0 g, Fiber: 3 g

---

INGREDIENTS

- ½ cup of pineapple chunks
- 1 cup of blueberries: frozen
- ½ cup of cucumber
- ½ cup of water
- ½ apple

INSTRUCTIONS

This recipe is for 2 servings only.

Add pineapple, cucumber, water, apple, and blueberries to a blending jar and blend to a smooth and thick texture. Serve it cool.

20. Avocado Smoothie

Preparation Time: 5 minutes

Total Time: 5 minutes

Servings: 2

Difficulty Level: Easy

Nutritional Information
Calories: 178 kcal, Protein: 5 g, Carbohydrates: 19 g, Fat: 9 g, Fiber: 5 g

INGREDIENTS

* 1 medium banana
* 1/2 medium avocado
* 1 cup of spinach
* 1–2 Medjool dates; (optional) pitted
* 1 cup of milk of your choice /or unsweetened almond milk

INSTRUCTIONS

This recipe is for 2 servings only.

In a blender, combine all the ingredients and mix until smooth. Serve right away with your preferred toppings. The smoothie is best served fresh, but it may be stored in an airtight container in the refrigerator for two days.

21. Pineapple Smoothie

Preparation Time: 5 minutes

Total Time: 5 minutes

Servings: 2

Difficulty Level: Easy

Nutritional Information
Calories: 181 kcal, Protein: 3 g, Carbohydrates: 33 g, Fat: 4 g, Fiber: 3 g

---

INGREDIENTS

- 1 frozen banana
- 1 cup of non-dairy milk
- 1 tbsp chia seeds
- 1 cup of pineapple chunks
- 1 cup of mango chunks

INSTRUCTIONS

This recipe is for 2 servings only.

In a high-powered blender, combine all the ingredients. Enjoy!

22. Strawberry Banana Smoothie

Preparation Time: 5 minutes

Total Time: 5 minutes

Servings: 2

Difficulty Level: Easy

Nutritional Information
Calories: 61 kcal, Protein: 3 g, Carbohydrates: 11 g, Fat: 1 g, Fiber: 2 g

---

INGREDIENTS

- ½ cup frozen or fresh strawberries
- 1 small ripe banana
- 5 ice cubes
- 1 cup of low-fat milk

INSTRUCTIONS

This recipe is for 2 servings only.

Put all the ingredients together in a blender, and blend until smooth for 3 to 4 minutes. If the mixture is too thick, add more milk. If the mixture is too thin, add less milk.

23. Anti-Acid Reflux Smoothie

Preparation Time: 5 minutes

Total Time: 5 minutes

Servings: 2

Difficulty Level: Easy

Nutritional Information
Calories: 125 kcal, Protein: 4 g, Carbohydrates: 21 g, Fat: 3 g, Fiber: 8 g

---

INGREDIENTS

- 1 stalk of celery; cut into chunks
- 1 red apple; cored & cut into chunks
- 1 small beet; peeled & cut into chunks
- 1 cup of carrot juice
- ½-inch of fresh ginger; peeled
- 1 cup of unsweetened almond milk

INSTRUCTIONS

This recipe is for 2 servings only.

Once everything is ready, combine everything in your blender and process until smooth. You'll need a higher powerful blender with this smoothie since using hard, fibrous veggies like carrots and beets.

24. Peach Smoothie

Preparation Time: 5 minutes

Total Time: 5 minutes

Servings: 2

Difficulty Level: Easy

Nutritional Information
Calories: 183 kcal, Protein: 8 g, Carbohydrates: 31 g, Fat: 3 g, Fiber: 4 g

INGREDIENTS

- 3/4 cup of fresh/frozen peaches
- 1/4 cup of non-fat Greek plain/vanilla yogurt
- 1/2 teaspoon of vanilla extract
- 3/4 cup of unsweetened almond milk/milk of choice
- 1/4 cup of frozen banana slices
- 1/2 tablespoon of honey and additional to taste
- 1/4 teaspoon of ground cinnamon
- A few ice cubes; optional
- Pinch of ground ginger

INSTRUCTIONS

This recipe is for 2 servings only.

Combine the yogurt, almond milk, peaches, banana, cinnamon, honey, vanilla, and ginger in a high-powered blender. Blend until completely smooth. (If you don't have a high-powered blender, gently add the fruit and extra almond milk to help the smoothie mix.) If you want the smoothie to be sweeter, taste it and add more honey if necessary. Blend in a few ice cubes if you want it thicker. Enjoy!

25. Green Smoothie

Preparation Time: 6 minutes

Total Time: 6 minutes

Servings: 2

Difficulty Level: Easy

Nutritional Information
Calories: 200 kcal, Protein: 9 g, Carbohydrates: 37 g, Fat: 1 g, Fiber: 5 g

---

INGREDIENTS

- 1 cup of packed baby spinach,
- 1 medium banana
- 1/4 cup of whole oats
- 1/2 cup of fat-free milk
- 3/4 cup of frozen mango
- 1/2 teaspoon of vanilla
- 1/4 cup of plain non-fat yogurt

INSTRUCTIONS

This recipe is for 2 servings only.

In a blender, purée all of the ingredients until smooth. Fill glasses with the smoothie and serve.

26. Guava Smoothie

Preparation Time: 5 minutes

Total Time: 5 minutes

Servings: 2

Difficulty Level: Easy

Nutritional Information
Calories: 116 kcal, Protein: 3 g, Carbohydrates: 26 g, Fat: 0 g, Fiber: 6 g

INGREDIENTS

- 1 cup of chopped guava, seeds removed.
- 1 cup of finely chopped baby spinach.
- 1 tsp of fresh ginger, grated.
- ½ medium-sized peeled and chopped mango.
- 1 banana, peeled and sliced.
- 2 cups of water

INSTRUCTIONS

This recipe is for 2 servings only.

After peeling the guava, cut it in half. Scope out the seeds and wash them. After cutting them into little pieces, set them aside. Rinse the baby spinach well under cold running water. Drain well and tear into small pieces, and set them aside. Bananas are peeled and chopped into small pieces and set aside. After peeling the mango, cut it into small pieces and set it aside. Puree the banana, guava, baby spinach, ginger, and mango until smooth in a juicer. Drizzle in the water a little until everything is creamy and smooth. Pour into serving glasses and chill for 20 mins before serving. Enjoy!

27. Healing Morning Smoothie

Preparation Time: 5 minutes

Total Time: 5 minutes

Servings: 2

Difficulty Level: Easy

Nutritional Information
Calories: 89 kcal, Protein: 3 g, Carbohydrates: 10 g, Fat: 4 g, Fiber: 6 g

---

INGREDIENTS

- 1 tablespoon of chia seeds
- 3/4 cup of berries/fruit of your choice
- 1 tablespoon of aloe vera
- 1/4 teaspoon of grated ginger
- 1 cup of coconut water
- 1/4 teaspoon of coconut oil

INSTRUCTIONS

This recipe is for 2 servings only.

In a blender, purée all of the ingredients until smooth. Fill glasses with the smoothie and serve.

28. Melon smoothie

Preparation Time: 5 minutes

Total Time: 5 minutes

Servings: 2

Difficulty Level: Easy

Nutritional Information
Calories: 126 kcal, Protein: 4 g, Carbohydrates: 14 g, Fat: 6 g, Fiber: 2 g

INGREDIENTS

- ¾ cup of chopped watermelon
- 1 cup of coconut water
- 1 tsp of flaxseeds
- 2 tbsp of natural; unsweetened peanut butter

INSTRUCTIONS

This recipe is for 2 servings only.

In a blender, purée all of the ingredients until smooth. Fill glasses with the smoothie and serve.

29. Banana blueberry smoothie

Preparation Time: 5 minutes

Total Time: 5 minutes

Servings: 2

Difficulty Level: Easy

Nutritional Information
Calories: 142 kcal, Protein: 6 g, Carbohydrates: 20 g, Fat: 4 g, Fiber: 3 g

---

INGREDIENTS

- ½ cup of blueberries
- 1 cup of unsweetened almond milk
- 1 banana
- ½ tsp of maple syrup
- 1 tsp of chia seeds
- 1 cup of spinach

INSTRUCTIONS

This recipe is for 2 servings only.

In a blender, purée all of the ingredients until smooth. Fill glasses with the smoothie and serve.

30. Pineapple Ginger Smoothie

Preparation Time: 5 minutes

Total Time: 5 minutes

Servings: 2

Difficulty Level: Easy

Nutritional Information
Calories: 179 kcal, Protein: 8 g, Carbohydrates: 24 g, Fat: 6 g, Fiber: 4 g

INGREDIENTS

- 1/4 cup of unsweetened almond milk and more
- 1/2 cup of nonfat plain Greek yogurt
- 1 frozen banana
- 1/2 teaspoon of freshly grated ginger or use 1/4 tsp of ground ginger
- 1 cup of fresh pineapple
- 2 teaspoons of chia seeds
- 1/2 teaspoon of ground turmeric

INSTRUCTIONS

This recipe is for 2 servings only.

In a blender, purée all of the ingredients until smooth. Fill glasses with the smoothie and serve.

Chapter 6
Snacks

Note: If you find any ingredients that trigger your acid reflux, feel free to omit or change that ingredient.

31. Baked French Fries

Preparation Time: 10 minutes

Total Time: 50 minutes

Servings: 4

Difficulty Level: Easy

Nutritional Information
Calories: 161 kcal, Protein: 3 g, Carbohydrates: 32 g, Fat: 3 g, Fibers: 5 g

---

INGREDIENTS

- 1 tablespoon of olive oil
- 4 medium russet potatoes
- 1/2 teaspoon of kosher salt

INSTRUCTIONS

This recipe is for 4 servings only. Leftover can be stored in an airtight container at room temperature for a day.

Set the oven to 400 degrees Fahrenheit. Prepare a baking sheet by lining it with parchment paper. Wash potatoes well to clear all dirt while keeping the skins intact. Using a long slicing motion, make thick slices. Cut again into sticks of the same length. Transfer to the baking sheet you have prepared. Salt the dish and drizzle it with olive oil. To evenly apply the seasoning, toss well. Bake for thirty-five to forty minutes while stirring once or twice. Once brown and crisp, take the food from the oven and let it cool before serving.

32. Persimmon Rounds

Preparation Time: 5 minutes

Total Time: 120 minutes

Servings: 6

Difficulty Level: Easy

Nutritional Information
Calories: 112 kcal, Protein: 1 g, Carbohydrates: 27 g, Fat: 0 g, Fibers: 6 g

INGREDIENTS

- 6 medium Fuyu persimmons

INSTRUCTIONS

This recipe is for 6 servings only. Leftover can be stored in an airtight container in the fridge for several days.

Preheat oven to 250°F. Crosswise, slice the persimmons into 1/4-inch-thick rounds. Spread the persimmons over two wire racks atop baking sheets. Bake for 1 1/2 to 2 hours, until the center, seems dry or the edges start to curl. Refrigerate in an airtight container.

33. Pumpkin Protein Bites

Preparation Time: 10 minutes

Total Time: 10 minutes

Servings: 6

Difficulty Level: Easy

Nutritional Information
Calories: 216 kcal, Protein: 7 g, Carbohydrates: 20 g, Fat: 12 g, Fibers: 3 g

---

INGREDIENTS

- 3 tbsp of raw honey or maple syrup
- 2/3 cup of sunflower seed butter
- 2/3 cup of pumpkin puree canned/ homemade
- 1/4 cup and 3-4 tbsp of coconut flour
- Chopped dried raisins or cranberries
- Pinch salt

INSTRUCTIONS

This recipe is for 6 servings only. Leftover can be stored in an airtight container in the fridge for 7 days.

Thoroughly combine the sunflower seed butter, pumpkin, and honey/maple syrup in a medium mixing bowl. Once mixed, add a tbsp of coconut flour at a time, carefully, until the mixture is thick enough to shape into balls - do not exceed 1/2 cup of coconut flour. Mix in the chopped raisins/cranberries, then form the mixture into small balls and chill until hard.

34. Pecan Pie Bites

Preparation Time: 15 minutes

Total Time: 25 minutes

Servings: 8

Difficulty Level: Easy

Nutritional Information
Calories: 242 kcal, Protein: 7 g, Carbohydrates: 22 g, Fat: 14 g, Fibers: 5 g

---

INGREDIENTS

Pie Crust

- 1 cup of pecans
- 2 cups of oats;
- ¼ cup of coconut oil; melted
- pinch of salt
- 1/4 cup of maple syrup

Caramel Filling

- 1/2 tsp of vanilla extract
- 6 tbsp of almond milk
- 1 cup of pitted Medjool dates
- pecans; to top
- pinch of salt

INSTRUCTIONS

This recipe is for 8 servings only. Leftover can be stored in an airtight container in the fridge for 3-4 days.

Preheat oven to 350 ° Fahrenheit. Mix the pecans, oats, maple syrup, coconut oil, and salt in a blender. Put a spoonful of mixture into a small tart pan (2 to 3 inches in diameter) and firmly push down with your palms. Bake for 7 to 9 minutes in the oven or till golden brown. Remove and let to cool. In a high-powered blender, combine the dates, vanilla, almond milk, and salt until smooth and creamy; scrape the sides of the food processor as necessary. Spread caramel filling over each pie using a knife, then top the pie with a pecan.

35. Honeycrisp Harvest Salad

Preparation Time: 10 minutes

Total Time: 30 minutes

Servings: 4

Difficulty Level: Easy

Nutritional Information
Calories: 343 kcal, Protein: 9 g, Carbohydrates: 34 g, Fat: 19 g, Fibers: 5 g

---

INGREDIENTS

For Roasted Vegetables:

- 1 teaspoon of salt
- 2 cups of cubed butternut squash
- 2 tablespoons of olive oil
- 2 cups of halved brussels sprouts

For Apple Cider Vinaigrette:

- 2 tablespoons of apple cider vinegar
- ½ cup of apple cider
- 1 tablespoon of maple syrup
- 1 tablespoon of Dijon mustard
- ½ teaspoon of ground cinnamon
- Salt; to taste
- ⅓ cup of extra-virgin olive oil

For Salad:

- ½ cup of dried cranberries
- 8 cups of mixed baby greens
- ½ cup of toasted walnuts/pecans; chopped
- 2 Honeycrisp apples; thinly sliced
- ¼ cup of pomegranate arils

INSTRUCTIONS

This recipe is for 4 servings only. Leftover can be stored in an airtight container in the fridge for one day.

For Roasted Vegetables:

Prepare a parchment paper-lined baking sheet and set the oven to 425°F. Spread the butternut squash & brussels sprouts in an equal layers on the baking sheet that has been prepared. Salt is then added after the olive oil is drizzled on top. Toss the vegetables to coat them uniformly with salt and oil. Bake for fifteen minutes, then toss and bake for 5-10 minutes. The brussels sprouts must be caramelized and crunchy in parts, while the squash must be soft. Put it aside to cool.

For Vinaigrette:

In a small saucepan, boil the apple cider while the vegetable roast. Simmer the cider until it is reduced to half, roughly 5 minutes. Combine the reduced cider, maple syrup, vinegar, mustard, and cinnamon in a medium bowl. Slowly pour some olive oil into the dish while continuously stirring the mixture. To taste, season with salt.

For Salad:

Add the greens, apples, almonds, dried cranberries, pomegranate arils, and roasted veggies to a large bowl. Add a little dressing, stir, and then taste the salad. As necessary, add extra dressing and a touch of salt. Serve right away.

36. White Bean & Avocado Toast

Preparation Time: 5 minutes

Total Time: 5 minutes

Servings: 1

Difficulty Level: Easy

Nutritional Information
Calories: 308 kcal, Protein: 15 g, Carbohydrates: 44 g, Fat: 8 g, Fiber: 4 g

---

INGREDIENTS

- ½ cup of canned white beans; rinsed and drained
- ¼ avocado; mashed
- Kosher salt; to taste
- 1 slice of whole-wheat bread; toasted

INSTRUCTIONS

This recipe is for 1 serving only.

Layer avocado & white beans on bread. Use a bit of salt to season the dish.

37. Watermelon Basil Salad

Preparation Time: 50 minutes

Total Time: 50 minutes

Servings: 4

Difficulty Level: Easy

Nutritional Information
Calories: 131 kcal, Protein: 7g, Carbohydrates: 19 g, Fat: 3 g, Fiber: 1 g

---

INGREDIENTS

- 4-ounce low-fat feta cheese
- ¼ cup of basil leaves
- 4 cups of watermelon; 1/2-inch cubes

INSTRUCTIONS

This recipe is for 4 servings only. Leftover can be stored in an airtight container in the fridge for one day.

Roll basil leaves into a log by stacking them on each other. Make thin ribbons by slicing them lengthwise. In a large bowl, combine cheese, watermelon and basil slices. Sprinkle salt over watermelon and toss to blend. Allow at least 30 minutes for the salad to chill before serving.

38. Avocado Hummus

Preparation Time: 10 minutes

Total Time: 10 minutes

Servings: 10

Difficulty Level: Easy

Nutritional Information
Calories: 133 kcal, Protein: 4 g, Carbohydrates: 9 g, Fat: 9 g, Fiber: 3 g

INGREDIENTS

- 1 ripe avocado; halved and pitted
- 1 (15 ounces) can of chickpeas; no-salt-added
- ¼ cup of low-fat yogurt
- 1 cup of fresh cilantro leaves
- ¼ cup of extra-virgin olive oil
- ½ teaspoon of salt
- 1 teaspoon of ground cumin

INSTRUCTIONS

This recipe is for 10 servings only. Leftover can be stored in an airtight container in the freezer for 2 weeks.

Setting aside two tbsp of the liquid, drain the chickpeas. Add the chickpeas and the liquid saved to a food processor. Add cilantro, avocado, yogurt, oil, cumin and salt. Blend until very smooth. Serve with vegetable chips, pita chips, or raw vegetables.

39. Carrot & Banana Muffins

Preparation Time: 10 minutes

Total Time: 60 minutes

Servings: 8

Difficulty Level: Easy

Nutritional Information
Calories: 218 kcal, Protein: 5 g, Carbohydrates: 36 g, Fat: 6 g, Fiber: 4 g

---

INGREDIENTS

- ¾ cup of whole-wheat flour
- 2 teaspoons baking powder
- 1 cup of raisins
- ¼ cup of canola oil
- 1 cup of oat bran
- ¾ cup all-purpose flour
- ½ cup of toasted wheat germ
- ¼ teaspoon salt
- ⅓ cup chopped walnuts
- 1 teaspoon of baking soda
- 2 teaspoons of ground cinnamon
- 1 cup of packed brown sugar
- 4 large egg whites
- 1 cup of mashed bananas; (2 medium bananas)
- ½ cup of low-fat milk
- 1 teaspoon vanilla extract
- 2 cups of shredded carrots; (4 medium carrots)

INSTRUCTIONS

This recipe is for 8 servings only. Leftover can be stored in an airtight container in the fridge for 3-4 day.

The oven should be heated to 400 degrees Fahrenheit. Coat 8 muffin cups of standard size (2 1/2 inches) with cooking spray. Put raisins in a small bowl, cover with boiling water, and let soak for 5 minutes. Drain and reserve. Whisk together all-purpose flour, whole-wheat flour, wheat germ, oat bran, baking soda, salt, cinnamon and baking powder in a large mixing bowl. In a medium bowl, whisk the egg whites until foamy. Whisk in the brown sugar until dissolved. Mix in milk, oil, bananas, and vanilla.

In the middle of the dry ingredients, make a well. Add the liquid ingredients and whisk until barely blended using a rubber spatula. Mix in carrots as well as the drained raisins carefully. Place the batter in the prepared pan & top with chopped nuts. Bake the muffins for 15 to 20 minutes or until the tops spring back after gently pressing. Allow the pan to cool for 5 minutes. Before serving, loosen the muffins' edges and place them on a wire rack to settle.

40. Hemp Banana & Peanut Butter

Preparation Time: 5 minutes

Total Time: 5 minutes

Servings: 1

Difficulty Level: Easy

Nutritional Information
Calories: 200 kcal, Protein: 5 g, Carbohydrates: 27 g, Fat: 8 g, Fiber: 4 g

INGREDIENTS

- 1 teaspoon of hemp seeds
- 1 banana
- 1 tablespoon of natural peanut butter

INSTRUCTIONS

This recipe is for 1 serving only.

Spread peanut butter on a banana and roll it with hemp hearts.

41. Yogurt Cereal Bowl

Preparation Time: 5 minutes

Total Time: 5 minutes

Servings: 2

Difficulty Level: Easy

Nutritional Information
Calories: 161 kcal, Protein: 14 g, Carbohydrates: 24 g, Fat: 1 g, Fiber: 6 g

---

INGREDIENTS

- ¼ cup of fresh raspberries
- ½ cup of mini, shredded-wheat cereal
- 1 cup of nonfat plain yogurt
- ¼ teaspoon of ground cinnamon
- 1 teaspoon of pumpkin seeds

INSTRUCTIONS

This recipe is for 2 serving only.

Combine shredded wheat, pumpkin seeds, raspberries, and cinnamon to yogurt in a dish.

42. Chickpea & Corn Sundal

Preparation Time: 5 minutes

Total Time: 15 minutes

Servings: 4

Difficulty Level: Easy

Nutritional Information
Calories: 196 kcal, Protein: 11 g, Carbohydrates: 29 g, Fat: 4 g, Fiber: 6 g

---

INGREDIENTS

- 1 large ear of fresh corn; boiled
- 2 cups of chickpeas; boiled
- 1/2 bunch of cilantro; chopped
- 2 sprigs of curry leaves
- 1 tbsp of black mustard seeds
- Salt to taste
- 1 tbsp of avocado oil

INSTRUCTIONS

This recipe is for 4 servings only. Leftover can be stored in an airtight container in the fridge for 1 to 2 day.

Using a knife, remove the kernels from the cob and put them aside. Warm the oil in a pan. Add mustard seeds when the oil is heated. Allow mustard seeds to begin to pop before adding curry leaves and stirring for around 30 seconds. Add the chickpeas & cook for about one minute. Mix in the cilantro, corn kernels, and salt until everything is cooked and combined. Serve warm or chilled.

43. Zucchini Carrot Celery Soup

Preparation Time: 5 minutes

Total Time: 35 minutes

Servings: 4

Difficulty Level: Easy

Nutritional Information
Calories: 87 kcal, Protein: 4 g, Carbohydrates: 11 g, Fat: 3 g, Fiber: 5 g

---

INGREDIENTS

- 3/4 tsp of turmeric
- 2 large zucchinis; washed and cubed
- 1 carrot, chopped
- 2 stalks of celery; sliced
- 1 inch of ginger, sliced
- 4-5 cups of Vegetable broth
- 1 tbsp of ground roasted cumin powder
- Salt, to taste
- 1 tbsp olive Oil

INSTRUCTIONS

This recipe is for 4 servings only. Leftover can be stored in an airtight container in the fridge for 3-4 day.

In a saucepan, heat 1 tablespoon of oil. Add the ginger slices and cook for about one minute. Add celery and carrots & sauté for around 5 minutes, until they wilt. Add turmeric, zucchini, and cumin. Cook for about five minutes or until the zucchini starts to shrink. Add four to five cups of broth. Cover and boil the soup for 20 minutes until all the vegetables are very soft. Cool the soup. You may add extra stock if necessary. Sprinkle chia seeds with your preferred toppings, like roasted broccoli & cauliflower florets.

44. Grape Apple Salad

Preparation Time: 10 minutes

Total Time: 2 hours 10 minutes

Servings: 8

Difficulty Level: Easy

Nutritional Information
Calories: 174 kcal, Protein: 5 g, Carbohydrates: 25 g, Fat: 6 g, Fiber: 3 g

---

INGREDIENTS

- ¼ cup of Honey
- 4 Diced apples (Gala)
- ½ cup of Chopped walnuts
- 1 cup of low-fat Greek yogurt
- 4 cups of seedless green grapes

INSTRUCTIONS

This recipe is for 8 servings only. Leftover can be stored in an airtight container in the fridge for one day.

Combine apples and grapes in a medium mixing bowl. Combine Greek yogurt and honey in a separate bowl. Pour the mixture into the bowl with the apples and grapes, and stir well. After covering, refrigerate for approximately 2 hours. Toss the salad with walnuts before serving.

Chapter 7
Lunch Recipes

Note: If you find any ingredients that trigger your acid reflux, feel free to omit or change that ingredient.

45. Chicken Salad

Preparation Time: 5 minutes

Total Time: 5 minutes

Servings: 2

Difficulty Level: Easy

Nutritional Information
Calories: 146 kcal, Protein: 18 g, Carbohydrates: 5 g, Fat: 6 g, Fibers: 2 g

---

INGREDIENTS

- 1 cup Lettuce, romaine, fresh, chopped,
- 1/4 cup green bell peppers, chopped
- 1/4 cup grated carrots
- 4 oz Chicken, broiler/fryer, breast, w/o skin
- 2 tbsp low-fat Cheddar Cheese, shredded
- 1 tsp olive oil
- 1 tbsp balsamic vinegar
- 1/4 tsp ground oregano

INSTRUCTIONS

This recipe is for 2 servings only.

Place the lettuce and vegetables on 2 plates. Top with equally divided chicken and cheese. Sprinkle with olive oil, vinegar, and oregano.

46. Zucchini Pasta with Ground Turkey and Fresh Peaches

Preparation Time: 5 minutes

Total Time: 20 minutes

Servings: 2

Difficulty Level: Easy

Nutritional Information
Calories: 191kcal, Protein: 13g, Carbohydrates: 19g, Fat: 7g, Fibers: 3g

---

INGREDIENTS

- Canola oil cooking spray
- 4 oz. lean ground turkey
- 3 cups zucchini noodles
- 1 medium carrot peeled and grated.
- 1 cup sliced peaches.

INSTRUCTIONS

This recipe is for 2 servings only.

Lightly spray a non-stick pan with the canola cooking spray, and heat over medium heat. Add the ground turkey, and sauté until the turkey is cooked through for 10-12 minutes. Toss the zucchini noodles with ground turkey, grated carrots, and sliced peaches. Allow to heat through or serve immediately. For a vegetarian take, toss zucchini noodles with grated carrots, juicy peaches, nectarines, and some blueberries.

47. Creamy Leek and Salmon Soup

Preparation Time: 5 minutes

Total Time: 30 minutes

Servings: 4

Difficulty Level: Medium

Nutritional Information
Calories: 386 kcal, Protein: 23 g, Carbohydrates: 15 g, Fat: 26 g, Fiber: 4 g

---

INGREDIENTS

- 4 leeks; washed, trimmed, & sliced into crescents
- 2 tbsp of avocado oil
- 2 tsp of dried thyme leaves
- 6 cups of seafood /chicken broth
- 1 lb. salmon, in bitesize pieces
- Salt to taste
- 1 3/4 cups of low-fat coconut milk

INSTRUCTIONS

This recipe is for 4 servings only. Leftover can be stored in an airtight container in the fridge for 1-2 day.

Heat avocado oil in a large pan or Dutch oven over low-medium heat. Add leeks and cook until slightly softened.

Add thyme and stock. Simmer for about 15 minutes, then season to taste with salt. Toss the salmon with the coconut milk in a pan. Return to low heat and simmer for approximately 10 minutes or until salmon is opaque and done. Serve immediately!

48. Shredded Chicken and Berry Salad

Preparation Time: 5 minutes

Total Time: 5 minutes

Servings: 2

Difficulty Level: Easy

Nutritional Information
Calories: 188 kcal, Protein: 23g, Carbohydrates: 15g, Fat: 4g, Fibers: 3g

---

INGREDIENTS

- 6 oz. Grilled chicken, shredded.
- 1 cup peeled and grated carrot.
- 1/2 cup shredded cucumbers
- 1/2 cup blueberries
- 1/2 cup strawberries, stems removed and halved.

INSTRUCTIONS

This recipe is for 2 servings only.

Combine the chicken, carrots, cucumbers, and berries in a salad bowl. Chill until ready to serve.

49. Vegan Tacos

Preparation time:20 minutes

Total Time: 20 mins

Servings: 4

Difficulty Level: Medium

Nutritional Information
Calories: 328 Kcal, Protein: 15 g, Carbohydrates: 31 g, Fat: 16 g, Fiber: 7 g

---

INGREDIENTS

- 2 tablespoons of tamari/soy sauce; reduced sodium.
- 1 (16 ounces) package of drained, crumbled extra-firm tofu; patted dry
- Pinch of salt
- 1 tablespoon of olive oil; extra-virgin
- 2 cups of iceberg lettuce, shredded.
- 1 ripe avocado
- 4 corn /flour tortillas; warmed.
- Pickled radishes; for garnish

INSTRUCTIONS

This recipe is for 4 servings only. Leftover can be stored in an airtight container in the fridge for 1-2 day.

In a medium mixing bowl, combine tamari/soy sauce and tofu. In a large nonstick pan, heat the oil over medium-high heat. Cook, stirring periodically until the tofu mixture is well browned; it will take about 8 to 10 minutes.

In a small bowl, mash the avocado with salt until smooth. In tortillas, serve the taco "meat", avocado crema, and lettuce. If preferred, serve with pickled radishes on top.

50. Shrimp Soup

Preparation Time: 20 minutes

Total Time: 25 minutes

Servings: 6

Difficulty Level: Medium

Nutritional Information
Calories: 220 Kcal, Protein: 19 g, Carbohydrates: 18 g, Fat: 8 g, Fiber: 3 g

---

INGREDIENTS

- 1 trimmed and coarsely chopped bunch of kale (16 cups)
- 4 teaspoons of olive oil; divided.
- 1 medium sweet red pepper; 3/4-inch pieces
- 1 can of rinsed and drained black-eyed peas (15-1/2 ounces),
- 3 cups of chicken broth; reduced sodium.
- 1/4 teaspoon of sea salt
- 1 pound of peeled and deveined uncooked shrimp (31-40 per pound),
- Minced fresh chives; optional.

INSTRUCTIONS

This recipe is for 6 servings only. Leftover can be stored in an airtight container in the fridge for one day.

Heat 2 teaspoons of oil in a 6-quart stockpot over medium-high heat. Cook and stir for 2 minutes after adding the shrimp. Cook for another 1-2 mins or until the shrimp turns pink. Remove it from the heat.

Heat the remaining oil in the same saucepan over medium-high heat. Add the red pepper and kale and cook, covered, for 8-10 minutes, until the kale is tender, stirring occasionally. Bring the broth to a boil. Add salt and peas, as well as the shrimp. Sprinkle chives on top of each serving if desired.

51. Chicken Salad Sandwich

Preparation Time: 10 minutes

Total Time: 30 minutes

Servings: 4

Difficulty Level: Medium

Nutritional Information
Calories: 330 Kcal, Protein: 29 g, Carbohydrates: 40 g, Fat: 6 g, Fiber: 2 g

---

INGREDIENTS

- 2/3 cup of low-fat ricotta cheese
- 1-pound skinless, boneless chicken breasts
- 1 1/2 teaspoons of dill
- 8 slices of whole bread
- 1/4 teaspoon of salt

INSTRUCTIONS

This recipe is for 4 servings only. Leftover can be stored in an airtight container in the fridge for one day.

In a saucepan of water, place the chicken breasts. Boil it, then lower it to a low heat setting. Cook until the chicken is no longer pink and the internal temperature reaches 170°F. It will take approximately 18-20 minutes.

Allow cooked chicken breasts to cool on a dish. To speed up the chilling process, cut each one in half. In a food processor, combine the cooked chicken breasts. Pulse the chicken a few times until it's finely chopped. Add ricotta cheese, salt, and dill. Stir. The bread should be toasted.

On 4 slices of bread, spread the chicken salad, then top with the remaining slices. If desired, garnish with cucumber slices and lettuce.

52. Carrot Ginger Soup

Preparation Time: 10 minutes

Total Time: 40 minutes

Servings: 6

Difficulty Level: Easy

> **Nutritional Information**
> Calories: 199 kcal, Protein: 5 g, Carbohydrates: 29 g, Fat: 7 g, Fiber: 7 g

INGREDIENTS

* 2 pounds peeled and chopped carrots,
* 1 tablespoon of grated fresh ginger,
* 1/2 teaspoon of turmeric
* 1 (15-oz) can of unsweetened almond milk; divided
* 1 teaspoon of ground cumin
* 1 1/2 teaspoons of sea salt; to taste.
* 4-5 cups of vegetable broth; low sodium

INSTRUCTIONS

This recipe is for 6 servings only. Leftover can be stored in an airtight container in the fridge for 2-3 day.

Add 1/2 cup of almond milk, carrots, grated ginger, cumin and turmeric, in a large sauce-pan, and sauté over medium heat until carrots soften, and everything is aromatic, approximately 8 minutes. You can speed up the process by covering the pot and stirring occasionally.

Add vegetable broth and remaining almond milk. Raise the heat to be high and bring the mixture to a full boil. Reduce to low heat and cover, and cook for about 20 to 30 minutes or until carrots are tender.

Transfer everything to a blender and mix until smooth (this may need to be done in stages). Let the steam escape by gently opening the steam vent at the top of the lid, then mix at medium speed.

Unless the soup is already at the appropriate temperature, return the smooth carrot soup to the saucepan and cook for a few minutes. If you must reheat the soup on the stove, do it carefully; else, your tasty soup will turn into a cauldron of boiling, spurting lava.

Serve with a dollop of no-fat yogurt, fresh cilantro and sesame seeds.

53. Chicken with Green Vegetables

Preparation Time: 10 minutes

Total Time: 45 minutes

Servings: 3

Difficulty Level: Medium

Nutritional Information
Calories: 280 kcal, Protein: 32 g, Carbohydrates: 7 g, Fat: 14 g, Fiber: 3 g

---

INGREDIENTS

- ½ cup of trimmed asparagus spears
- 1-pound boneless and skinless chicken breasts (cubed)
- ½ cup of green beans (trimmed)
- 1 tablespoon of olive oil
- ¼ cup of chopped basil leaves(fresh)
- 1 cup of chicken broth
- Salt to taste
- 1 cup of coconut milk (unsweetened)

INSTRUCTIONS

This recipe is for 3 servings only. Leftover can be stored in an airtight container in the fridge for one day.

Heat the oil in a skillet over medium flame, add the chicken and cook for 8-10 minutes. Add chicken broth and coconut milk and boil it. Lower the heat and simmer for 8-10 minutes. Cook for around 4-5 minutes after adding the green beans, asparagus and salt. Serve once it's done.

54. Creamy Chicken Soup with Cauliflower

Preparation Time: 10 minutes

Total Time: 45 minutes

Servings: 8

Difficulty Level: Easy

Nutritional Information
Calories: 150 kcal, Protein: 18g, Carbohydrates: 9 g, Fat: 5g, Fibers: 3g

---

INGREDIENTS

- 1 teaspoon extra-virgin olive oil
- 1 medium potato
- 1 carrot diced.
- 2 cups of low-sodium chicken broth
- 1 celery stalk, diced.
- 1 ½ pounds cooked chicken breast; (3 or 4 medium), diced.
- 2 cups of water
- 1 cup of fresh spinach, chopped.
- 1 teaspoon diced thyme
- 2 cups of nonfat or 1 % milk
- 2 ½ cups of fresh cauliflower florets

INSTRUCTIONS

This recipe is for 8 servings only. Leftover can be stored in an airtight container in the fridge for 2-3 day.

Place a wide soup pot over medium-high heat. Add the carrot and celery, and sauté until tender, 3 to 5 minutes. Add the broth, chicken breast, potato, thyme, water, and cauliflower. Boil it, reduce heat to medium-low & cook uncovered for 30 minutes. Add the fresh spinach and stir until wilted, about 5 minutes. Stir in the milk, then serve immediately.

55. Fish Sandwich

Preparation Time: 20 minutes

Total Time: 65 minutes

Servings: 2

Difficulty Level: Medium

Nutritional Information
Calories: 485 Kcal, Protein: 34 g, Carbohydrates: 58 g, Fat: 13 g, Fiber: 3 g

---

INGREDIENTS

For the fish:

- ½ cup of whole flour
- 2 halibut filets; thawed.
- ½ tsp. of parsley
- ½ tsp. of salt
- 1 tbsp olive oil

For the sandwich:

- ½ sliced yellow bell pepper,
- 4 slices of whole bread
- 1 sliced cucumber,
- 1/3 cup of spinach

INSTRUCTIONS

This recipe is for 2 servings only.

Preheat the oven to 350 degrees Fahrenheit. Using parchment paper, line a baking sheet. Combine flour, parsley, and salt in a mixing bowl. To remove the skin from the halibut, use kitchen scissors. Place one halibut fillet at a time in the flour mixture in the mixing bowl. Cover the fillet with a small layer of olive oil and pat it onto the fish with your palms. Place the fillets on the baking sheet that has been prepared and bake the fish for 20-25 minutes or until golden brown. Take the fish out of the oven. Place the sliced bell pepper on the bottom of the sandwiches, followed by the sliced cucumber, spinach and baked fish.

56. Chicken Lettuce Wraps

Preparation Time: 15 minutes

Total Time: 30 minutes

Servings: 2

Difficulty Level: Easy

Nutritional Information
Calories: 206 kcal, Protein: 24 g, Carbohydrates: 7 g, Fat: 9 g, Fiber: 2 g

---

INGREDIENTS

For Chicken:
- 1 tablespoon avocado oil
- ½ teaspoon fresh ginger, minced.
- ½ pound ground chicken
- Salt to taste.

For Wraps:
- 5 romaine lettuce leaves
- 1/2 cup carrot peeled and julienned.
- ½ tablespoons fresh parsley, chopped finely.

INSTRUCTIONS

This recipe is for 2 servings only.

Heat the oil over medium heat in a skillet and sauté ginger for about 4-5 minutes. Add the ground chicken and salt and cook over medium-high heat for about 7-9 minutes, breaking the meat into smaller pieces with a wooden spoon. Remove from the heat and set aside to cool. Arrange the lettuce leaves onto serving plates. Place the cooked chicken over each lettuce leaf and top with carrot and cilantro.

57. Chickpea and Garden Pea Stew

Preparation Time: 10 minutes

Total Time: 40 minutes

Servings: 4

Difficulty Level: Medium

> **Nutritional Information**
> Calories: 186 kcal, Protein: 11 g, Carbohydrates: 31 g, Fat: 2 g, Fiber: 6 g

INGREDIENTS

- 1/2 cup reduced-sodium chicken stock.
- 1 cup canned chickpeas drained and rinsed.
- 1 cup frozen green peas, defrosted.
- 1 tbsp. Fresh cilantro, chopped.

INSTRUCTIONS

This recipe is for 4 servings only. Leftover can be stored in an airtight container in the fridge for 2-3 day.

Put the chicken stock in a soup pot and boil. Reduce the heat and add the chickpeas. Simmer covered for 15 minutes or until the chickpeas are softened. Add the green peas and cilantro, and heat through for 5 minutes. Serve hot.

58. Chicken and Lotus Root Soup

Preparation Time: 10 minutes

Total Time: 6-7 hours

Servings: 2

Difficulty Level: Easy

Nutritional Information
Calories: 199 kcal, Protein: 22g, Carbohydrates: 21g, Fat: 3g, Fibers: 6g

INGREDIENTS

- 3 1/2 oz. lotus roots
- 3 oz. skinless chicken breast
- 1 cup reduced-sodium chicken stock.
- 1 cup water
- 1/2 carrot, diced.

INSTRUCTIONS

This recipe is for 2 servings only.

Combine the ingredients in a slow cooker. Set on LOW for 6-7 hours. Serve piping hot.

Chapter 8
Dinner Recipes

Note: If you find any ingredients that trigger your acid reflux, feel free to omit or change that ingredient.

59. Maple BBQ Salmon

Preparation Time: 15 minutes

Total Time: 45 minutes

Servings: 2

Difficulty Level: Medium

Nutritional Information
Calories: 603 kcal, Protein: 32 g, Carbohydrates: 67 g, Fat: 23 g, Fibers: 1 g

---

INGREDIENTS

- 1 tablespoon of brown sugar (or maple)
- 1 pound salmon filets
- ½ teaspoon of salt
- 2 to 3 tablespoons of maple syrup
- ¼ teaspoon of cumin

Couscous
- 1 ¼ cups of chicken or water or vegetable stock
- 1 cup of uncooked pearl couscous
- pinch of salt
- 1 tablespoon of unsalted butter

INSTRUCTIONS

This recipe is for 2 servings only. Leftover can be stored in an airtight container in the fridge for one day.

Preheat oven to 400 °F. Place the fish on a sheet pan. Mix the sugar, salt and cumin in a small bowl. Spread it evenly on the salmon fillets. Drizzle each fillet with maple syrup with a spoon to distribute it evenly throughout the fillet. Roast for about 10 and 15 mins, or until the salmon flakes easily with a fork. When it is taken out of the oven, you may, if wanted, brush it with a little extra maple syrup. Top using chopped chives. Serve warm with sauce.

Couscous

In a large saucepan heated over medium heat, melt the butter. Mix in couscous until evenly coated, then sauté for two to three mins, occasionally stirring, until couscous is toasted. Bring this to a boil after adding the chicken stock and salt. Once boiling, decrease the temperature to a simmer, then cover. Cook for 15 mins or until the fluid has been absorbed. Turn off the heat and serve with the salmon on the top.

60. Crispy Broiled Haddock with Broccolini

Preparation Time: 5 minutes

Total Time: 15 minutes

Servings: 2

Difficulty Level: Easy

Nutritional Information
Calories: 312 kcal, Protein: 35 g, Carbohydrates: 7 g, Fat: 16 g, Fibers: 6 g

INGREDIENTS

* 1 bunch of Broccolini; (trimmed)
* 2 Haddock Fillets; (5 ounces each)
* 2 tbsps. Of Avocado Oil
* 1/2 tsp of Sea Salt
* 1 tsp of Dried Thyme

INSTRUCTIONS

This recipe is for 2 servings only.

Adjust the oven rack to be 6 inches from the top and warm the broiler. Line a baking sheet with parchment paper or a silicone baking mat. Place all haddock fillets & Broccolini on a tray & cover with avocado oil in a uniform layer. Season with salt and thyme. Approximately six to eight minutes under a hot broiler will allow the fish to flake easily with a fork. Enjoy!

61. Root Vegetables and Apricot Chicken Thighs

Preparation Time: 15 minutes

Total Time: 32 minutes

Servings: 3

Difficulty Level: Easy

Nutritional Information
Calories: 308 kcal, Protein: 25 g, Carbohydrates: 14 g, Fat: 17 g, Fibers: 4 g

---

INGREDIENTS

- 20 ounces Organic Skinless Boneless Chicken Thighs
- 1 tablespoon of olive oil
- Kosher salt; to taste
- 1 teaspoon of fresh, finely chopped thyme
- 1/4 cup of apricot preserves
- 2/3 cup of chicken broth; low sodium
- 1 cup of diced carrots
- 2 tablespoons of Dijon mustard
- 1 teaspoon of fresh, finely chopped sage
- 1 cup of diced parsnips
- 1 cup of diced rutabaga
- 1 teaspoon of fresh, finely chopped rosemary

INSTRUCTIONS

This recipe is for 3 servings only. Leftover can be stored in an airtight container in the fridge for one day.

In a large skillet, heat the oil over medium heat. Salt the chicken thighs before adding them to a heated skillet. Cook each side for about 3 to 4 minutes until almost golden brown. At this time, the chicken won't be entirely cooked. Place the chicken on a platter after removing it from the pan. Combine chicken broth, apricot preserves, and Dijon in small bowl. Set aside. In a pan, sauté the carrots, parsnips, & rutabaga for 4-5 minutes with salt. Herbs should be added and cooked for another minute.

Return the chicken to a skillet and pour the apricot mixture over it. Turn the heat down to medium, covering with a lid or foil, and cook for an additional 7 to 8 minutes or until the chicken is cooked. Once the chicken thighs are cooked, check for seasoning and sprinkle a portion of the sauce. Add more fresh herbs, then serve.

62. Banh mi bowls & sticky tofu

Preparation Time: 15 minutes

Total Time: 30 minutes

Servings: 2 bowls

Difficulty Level: Easy

Nutritional Information
Calories: 533 kcal, Protein: 23 g, Carbohydrates: 54 g, Fat: 25 g, Fibers: 8 g

---

INGREDIENTS

Sticky Tofu:

- 2 tbsp of avocado oil
- 1 pack of tofu
- 1 tbsp of soy sauce
- 2 tbsp of hoisin sauce

Bowls:

- 1/2 cup of thinly sliced /shredded carrots
- 1 handful of cilantro; chopped
- 1/2 cup of shredded red cabbage/pickled red cabbage
- sesame seeds; for topping
- 1 cup of shredded lettuce
- 1/2 cup of thinly sliced cucumbers
- 1/2 pack of rice noodles
- 1/2 avocado, sliced

INSTRUCTIONS

This recipe is for 2 servings only.

Let's begin by making the sticky tofu. Cube the tofu and set it in a skillet over medium-high heat with the oil. Let the cubes turn brown for roughly three to five minutes, then turn each side to brown. Turn off the heat and stir with hoisin sauce and soy sauce when each side turns golden brown and crispy. Prepare the rice noodles as per the instructions on the box. The noodles should be placed at the bottom of your bowl, followed by tofu, carrots, lettuce, cucumber, cilantro, avocado, red cabbage, and sesame seeds. Add more soy sauce & hoisin sauce. Enjoy!

63. Honey Mustard Chicken & Potatoes

Preparation Time: 10 minutes

Total Time: 60 minutes

Servings: 3

Difficulty Level: Easy

Nutritional Information
Calories: 407 kcal, Protein: 29 g, Carbohydrates: 39 g, Fat: 15 g, Fibers: 6 g

---

INGREDIENTS

- 8 chicken thighs, bone-in
- 1 teaspoon of olive oil
- ½ teaspoon of sea salt
- 1 head of broccoli; chopped into florets
- 4 red potatoes; chopped

Honey Mustard Sauce

- 2 tablespoons of grainy mustard
- ¼ cup each; honey and Dijon mustard
- ¼ cup of water

INSTRUCTIONS

This recipe is for 3 servings only. Leftover can be stored in an airtight container in the fridge for one day.

Preheat the oven to 400 °F. Heat oil in a big oven-safe skillet over medium-high heat. Add the chicken with the skin up. The skin is seasoned with sea salt. Cook the chicken for 5 minutes, then turn it over and cook until the skin is golden, approximately 5 more minutes. While the chicken is cooking, cut the potatoes.

Remove the skillet from heat and transfer the chicken onto a bowl. Whisk together all the ingredients for the sauce in a saucepan. Stir the potatoes into the sauce until they are well covered. Nestle the chicken amongst the potatoes & pour any collected liquids (from the dish the chicken has been in) back into the pan.

Put the skillet in the oven and cook it for thirty minutes. Carefully remove your pan from the oven and add the broccoli. Return the pan to the oven for fifteen to twenty minutes until the potatoes are tender.

64. Quinoa Crusted Salmon

Preparation Time: 5 minutes

Total Time: 15 minutes

Servings: 2

Difficulty Level: Easy

Nutritional Information
Calories: 389 kcal, Protein: 32 g, Carbohydrates: 22 g, Fat: 19 g, Fibers: 2 g

---

INGREDIENTS

- 1 egg
- chives for garnish
- 12 oz. salmon fillets; 2, 6 oz. fillets
- ½ teaspoon of parsley
- 3 tablespoons of breadcrumbs;
- ½ teaspoon of salt
- 3 tablespoons of quinoa uncooked; rinsed

INSTRUCTIONS

This recipe is for 2 servings only.

In one dish, whisk the egg, and in another, add the uncooked quinoa, breadcrumbs, salt, and parsley.

Heat 1-2 tablespoons of oil over medium heat in a nonstick pan. Coat all salmon fillets on both sides by dipping them first in the egg mixture and later in the quinoa mixture. Place the salmon skin-side into the pan and cover it with the lid. Cook fish for 5 to 6 minutes, then turn and cook for 1 to 2 minutes. Enjoy salmon topped with fresh chives.

65. Baked Chicken Meatballs

Preparation Time: 10 minutes

Total Time: 30 minutes

Servings: 4

Difficulty Level: Easy

Nutritional Information
Calories: 236 kcal, Protein: 20 g, Carbohydrates: 8 g, Fat: 14 g, Fibers: 1 g

---

INGREDIENTS

- 1/2 cup of grated Parmesan
- 1-pound ground turkey or chicken
- 1 egg
- 2 tablespoons of olive oil (optional)
- 1/2 teaspoon of salt
- 1/2 cup of panko breadcrumbs
- additional seasonings; optional

INSTRUCTIONS

This recipe is for 4 servings only. Leftover can be stored in an airtight container in the fridge for 2-3 day.

Preheat oven to 400 °F. Prepare a baking sheet using aluminium foil and cooking spray. Combine all of the ingredients in a bowl. Shape this mixture into about thirty small balls. Arrange on a baking sheet. Bake for 25-30 mins. ENJOY!

66. Balsamic Chicken

Preparation Time: 10 minutes

Total Time: 45 minutes

Servings: 2

Difficulty Level: Medium

Nutritional Information
Calories: 524 kcal, Protein: 31 g, Carbohydrates: 62 g, Fat: 17 g, Fibers: 4 g

---

INGREDIENTS

- 2 tablespoons of balsamic vinegar
- 1/3 cup of honey
- 1 tablespoon of olive oil
- salt; to taste
- 1 1/2 teaspoons of dried Italian seasoning
- 4 skin-on, bone-in chicken thighs
- 1-pound red potatoes; small, halved
- 1 pound asparagus stalks; trimmed
- cooking spray
- 2 tablespoons of chopped parsley

INSTRUCTIONS

This recipe is for 2-4 servings only. Leftover can be stored in an airtight container in the fridge for 1-2 day.

Preheat oven to 425 °F. Coat foil is used to line a baking sheet with cooking spray. Place the chicken thighs in the skillet. Liberally season the chicken with salt. Mix honey, balsamic vinegar, & Italian spice using a whisk. Combine the potatoes with olive oil and salt in a large bowl. Toss to mix. Place these potatoes around chicken thighs. Brush chicken with half of the balsamic mixture. Bake for twenty minutes. Coat the chicken with the remaining glaze, then add asparagus to a pan. Asparagus is seasoned with salt. Another 10 to 15 minutes cooking, or until the chicken is cooked through and the potatoes & asparagus are soft. After garnishing with parsley, serve.

67. Chicken Stir Fry

Preparation Time: 15 minutes

Total Time: 30 minutes

Servings: 5

Difficulty Level: Easy

Nutritional Information
Calories: 407 kcal, Protein: 23 g, Carbohydrates: 48 g, Fat: 13 g, Fibers: 4 g

---

INGREDIENTS

- 1/2 cup of homemade or store-bought chicken broth
- 3 tablespoons plus 1 teaspoon of olive oil
- 1 teaspoon of cornstarch
- 1 tablespoon of sherry cooking wine or use rice wine
- 1/4 cup of low-sodium soy sauce
- 4 oz. green onion; 1" in length
- 8 - 10 oz. rice noodles/ thin spaghetti
- 1 red bell pepper; sliced
- 4 oz. snow peas
- 1 teaspoon of grated fresh ginger
- splash of sesame oil
- 6 boneless skinless chicken thighs; bite-size pieces

INSTRUCTIONS

This recipe is for 5 servings only. Leftover can be stored in an airtight container in the fridge for 1-2 day.

Bring to a boil a big saucepan of salted water. Cook the noodles according to the directions on the box. Drain, then combine with 1 tsp of olive oil. Set aside. Mix chicken broth, sherry wine, soy sauce, and cornstarch in a small mixing dish. Stir, then put aside. Heat 1 tbsp of olive oil in a large pan over medium-high heat. Add sliced red bell pepper, grated ginger, snow peas, and green onion. Cook for 3 to 5 mins or until tender. Place onto a plate. Heat two tbsp. of olive oil over medium/high heat in a skillet. Separate the chicken into two batches and stir-fry each batch for about five minutes or until the chicken is fully done. Stir-fry the veggies, noodles, and broth mixture for two minutes or until the noodles are well warm. Season with a dash of sesame oil & soy sauce, and serve warm. Take a fork and dig in!

68. Summer Squash Pasta

Preparation Time: 5 minutes

Total Time: 20 minutes

Servings: 2

Difficulty Level: Easy

Nutritional Information
Calories: 508 kcal, Protein: 24 g, Carbohydrates: 67 g, Fat: 16 g, Fibers: 3 g

---

INGREDIENTS

- ¼ cup of pine nuts
- 6 ounces of pasta
- 2 tablespoons of unsalted butter
- 1 zucchini squash, small; sliced into rounds
- kosher salt
- 1 summer squash, small; sliced into rounds
- ¼ cup of fresh basil leaves
- 4 ounces low-fat mozzarella cheese; crumbled

INSTRUCTIONS

This recipe is for 2 servings only. Leftover can be stored in an airtight container in the fridge for 1-2 day.

Bring a saucepan of salt water to a boil, then cook the pasta as directed. While the pasta cooks heat a pan over medium-low heat. Add pine nuts. Toss and stir until golden and aromatic, roughly 5 to 6 mins. Remove quickly from heat. In a skillet heated over medium heat, melt the butter. Constantly whisk it until brown pieces emerge just on the bottom, and the butter becomes golden. Add the squash rounds, stir to coat, and simmer for 5 minutes or until the zucchini has softened. It is seasoned with salt. Pasta should be done by now; therefore, add it to the zucchini in the pan. Reduce the heat to a low setting. Make sure the pasta & squash are well combined and topped with a dab of butter before serving. Crumble mozzarella cheese into the salad and stir well. Add the pine nuts. Add the fresh basil & serve right away.

69. Sweet Potato Noodles

Preparation Time: 5 minutes

Total Time: 20 minutes

Servings: 4

Difficulty Level: Easy

Nutritional Information
Calories: 315 kcal, Protein: 26 g, Carbohydrates: 28 g, Fat: 11 g, Fibers: 7 g

---

INGREDIENTS

- 2 big handfuls of baby spinach
- 1 lb. of ground turkey
- 3-4 tbsp of chicken or veggie broth
- 6–7 oz sweet potato noodles
- 1 tbsp of avocado oil or olive oil
- Himalayan salt; to taste
- 1 tsp. of ground cumin

INSTRUCTIONS

This recipe is for 4 servings only. Leftover can be stored in an airtight container in the fridge for 1-2 day.

In a skillet, heat the oil over medium heat. Add ground turkey, salt, cumin, & pepper to the skillet. Sweet potato noodles are added halfway while cooking the ground turkey. Cook for 5 to 7 minutes while stirring occasionally. Adding a few tablespoons of broth will keep the noodles from sticking. Add baby spinach and continue cooking for a few minutes or until it has wilted.

70. Turmeric Coconut Cauliflower Bowls

Preparation Time: 10 minutes

Total Time: 30 minutes

Servings: 4

Difficulty Level: Easy

Nutritional Information
Calories: 416 kcal, Protein: 13 g, Carbohydrates: 81 g, Fat: 4 g, Fibers: 6 g

INGREDIENTS

- 2 cups of Plain Coconut Milk
- 2 cups of Jasmine Rice; (dry, rinsed)
- 1 tsp of Turmeric
- 1 tsp of Sea Salt
- 1 head of cauliflower; (chopped into florets)
- 1/4 cup of cilantro (chopped)

INSTRUCTIONS

This recipe is for 4 servings only. Leftover can be stored in an airtight container in the fridge for 1-2 day.

Follow the instructions on the box while preparing jasmine rice. While the rice is cooking, heat the coconut milk, salt and turmeric in a pan over medium heat. Stir together and simmer over low heat.

Once bubbles form within the sauce, add cauliflower florets and simmer covered for fifteen to twenty minutes or until the sauce reaches the desired consistency. Divide the rice into bowls. Serve with cilantro and cauliflower. Enjoy!

71. Tomato Sauce-Free Lasagna

Preparation Time: 25 minutes

Total Time: 60 minutes

Servings: 5

Difficulty Level: Easy

Nutritional Information
Calories: 366 kcal, Protein: 22 g, Carbohydrates: 29 g, Fat: 18 g, Fibers: 2 g

---

INGREDIENTS

- Nonstick cooking spray
- 12 ounces lasagna noodles; wide
- 12 ounces lean ground beef (ground sirloin or ground round)
- 1/4 cup of low-fat cream cheese
- 1/2 cup of low-sodium beef broth
- 1 1/4 cups of skim milk / 1% milk; divided
- 2 tablespoons of butter
- 1 tablespoon of all-purpose flour
- 1/2 cup of Parmesan cheese, high-quality; shredded
- 1 1/2 cups of skim mozzarella cheese; grated
- Salt; to taste

INSTRUCTIONS

This recipe is for 5 servings only. Leftover can be stored in an airtight container in the fridge for 2-3 day.

Preheat oven to 375 degrees Fahrenheit. Bring to a boil a big saucepan of salted water. Cook the lasagna noodles according to the directions on the box or until tender. Drain well. While the noodles simmer, proceed with the other steps of the recipe.

Coat a big, nonstick skillet with cooking spray. Cook the ground beef at medium heat until no longer pink. Discard the liquid. Place the browned meat and beef broth in a large bowl. Blend.

In a small mixing bowl, combine cream cheese, roughly a quarter of the milk, and flour to prepare the low-fat Alfredo sauce. Beat until well mixed. Pour the remaining milk in slowly and mix until smooth. Melt butter over medium heat in a big nonstick saucepan. Add the combo of milk and cream cheese. Cook for about four minutes, stirring continuously until the sauce thickens.

Stir Parmesan cheese into the dish. Add salt to taste. Turn the heat off. Spread 1 cup of low-fat Alfredo sauce on the bottom of a 13x9-inch baking dish. Cover the sauce with three pieces of cooked lasagna noodles. Spread over the top half of the beef mixture. Lay down three more lasagna noodles. Top with the leftover beef mixture. Then, layer the remaining three lasagna noodle strips.

Spread the leftover Alfredo sauce on top. Sprinkle mozzarella cheese over the top. Bake between 25 and 35 minutes until bubbling and golden brown. Let it cool for three to four minutes before serving.

72. Butternut Squash Buckwheat Bowl

Preparation Time: 5 minutes

Total Time: 35 minutes

Servings: 2

Difficulty Level: Easy

Nutritional Information
Calories: 338 kcal, Protein: 16 g, Carbohydrates: 64 g, Fat: 2 g, Fibers: 6 g

INGREDIENTS

- 1 cup of buckwheat groats
- 2 cups of water
- 1 cup of butternut squash; diced
- 1 cup of kale leaves; chopped
- 1/2 cup of mushrooms; sliced
- 1 tsp of sea salt

INSTRUCTIONS

This recipe is for 2 servings only.

In a saucepan of average size, boil the water. Turn down the heat & add the buckwheat after the liquid has boiled. Cook for fifteen to twenty minutes or until water has been absorbed.

Sauté the butternut squash, kale, sea salt, mushrooms, and 1/3 cup of water in a separate skillet over medium heat. Stir constantly for 15 minutes or until well cooked. (Cooking with the lid on for a few minutes may prevent sticking). Place the prepared buckwheat in bowls. Serve with kale mixture and spices.

73. Sauerkraut Crusted Salmon and Greens

Preparation Time: 5 minutes

Total Time: 25 minutes

Servings: 2

Difficulty Level: Easy

Nutritional Information
Calories: 435 kcal, Protein: 34 g, Carbohydrates: 13 g, Fat: 28 g, Fibers: 6 g

---

INGREDIENTS

* 1 pound Salmon Fillet
* 2 tbsp of Whole Grain Mustard
* 1/4 cup of Sauerkraut
* 2 tsps. Of Avocado Oil
* 1/2 cucumber; (sliced)
* 4 cups of Mixed Greens

INSTRUCTIONS

This recipe is for 2 servings only.

Preheat oven to 370 degrees F. Combine the sauerkraut & mustard in a bowl. Spread the mixture over the flesh part of the fish and firmly press. In an oven-safe pan, heat the oil over medium heat. Cook the fish for eight minutes with the flesh side down. Flip the salmon. Transfer the dish to the oven to bake for eight minutes more. On plates, place the mixed greens & cucumbers. Enjoy the dish with salmon on top!

Chapter 9
Desserts

Note: If you find any ingredients that trigger your acid reflux, feel free to omit or change that ingredient.

74. Cranberry Pistachio Oatmeal Cookies

Preparation Time: 5 minutes

Total Time: 15 minutes

Servings: 2 dozen

Difficulty Level: Easy

Nutritional Information
Calories: 109 kcal, Protein: 2 g, Carbohydrates: 14 g, Fat: 5 g, Fibers: 1 g

---

INGREDIENTS

- 1/2 cup unsalted butter; softened
- 3/4 cup all-purpose flour
- 1/2 teaspoon baking soda
- 1/2 cup brown sugar
- 1/2 teaspoon baking powder
- 1 egg
- 1/2 teaspoon ground cinnamon
- 1 1/2 cups regular oats
- pinch of salt
- 1/2 teaspoon vanilla extract
- 1/4 cup pistachios
- 3/4 cup dried cranberries

INSTRUCTIONS

This recipe is for 24 servings only. Leftover can be stored in an airtight container in the fridge for 4-5 day.

Heat the oven to 350 degrees Fahrenheit. Mix oats, baking powder, cinnamon, baking soda, flour and salt in a large basin. In a mixer, cream together vanilla, butter, and brown sugar. Add in an egg. Mix until blended.

Slowly blend the oat flour mixture with the other ingredients using a stand mixer. Toss in the cranberries & pistachios carefully. Place 1 spoonful of cookie dough 2 inches apart on a baking sheet coated with a silicone mat/parchment paper. Bake for 8-10 mins. Take out of the oven and place on a cooling rack.

75. Pecan Cookies

Preparation Time: 10 minutes

Total Time: 30 minutes

Servings: 10

Difficulty Level: Easy

Nutritional Information
Calories: 108 kcal, Protein: 4 g, Carbohydrates: 14 g, Fat: 4 g, Fibers: 2 g

---

INGREDIENTS

- 1/2 cup pecan butter
- 1 1/2 cup Kamut flour
- 6 tbsp. no-calorie sweetener (e.g., Splenda Brown Sugar Blend)
- 1/4 cup of low-fat almond milk
- 1 tsp. vanilla extract
- 1/2 tsp. salt

INSTRUCTIONS

This recipe is for 10 servings only. Leftover can be stored in an airtight container in the fridge for 4 day.

Preheat an oven to 350°F, and line a cookie sheet with parchment paper. Combine the pecan butter, Kamut flour, sweetener, almond milk, vanilla extract, & salt in a mixing bowl. Divide the dough into 10 cookies. Bake the cookies for 20 minutes. Transfer to a cookie rack to cool completely before serving.

76. Apple Cake

Preparation Time: 10 minutes

Total Time: 35 minutes

Servings: 2

Difficulty Level: Easy

Nutritional Information
Calories: 128 kcal, Protein: 5 g, Carbohydrates: 18 g, Fat: 4 g, Fibers: 3 g

INGREDIENTS

- 2 tbsp. whole meal plain flour
- 1/4 tbsp. granulated sweetener
- 1/2 tsp. ground cinnamon
- 1 1/2 tsp. baking powder
- 1 egg
- 1 tbsp. Vanilla skim milk/skim milk + 1 tsp. vanilla extract
- 1/2 tbsp. Low-fat butter, melted.
- 1/2 tbsp. applesauce
- 1 cup cooking apples, peeled, cored, and cut into thin slices.

INSTRUCTIONS

This recipe is for 2 servings only. Leftover can be stored in an airtight container in the fridge for 2-4 day.

Preheat the oven to 400°F, and lightly spray a mini-loaf tin with low-fat cooking spray.

To make the batter:

Mix the whole meal flour with sugar, ground cinnamon, and baking powder. Make a well in the center and add the egg, skim milk and vanilla extract. Stir in.

Stir in the melted low-fat butter and applesauce. Fold in the apple slices. Pour the batter into the tin and bake for 20 to 25 minutes until the cake has risen and is firm and golden. Allow the cake to cool slightly in the pan when it is done.

77. Pumpkin Cheesecake Bites

Preparation Time: 5 minutes

Total Time: 10 minutes

Servings: 1 dozen

Difficulty Level: Easy

Nutritional Information
Calories: 59 kcal, Protein: 4 g, Carbohydrates: 4 g, Fat: 3 g, Fibers: 0 g

---

INGREDIENTS

- 1/2 cup of low-fat ricotta cheese
- 1 block (8 oz.) of cream cheese; reduced fat
- 1/2 cup of pumpkin puree
- ½ tsp of pumpkin pie spice
- 2 tsp of vanilla
- ½ tsp of cinnamon
- 2 packages of Puff Pastry Small Cups
- 3 tablespoons of powdered sugar

INSTRUCTIONS

This recipe is for 12 servings only. Leftover can be stored in an airtight container in the fridge for 3-4 day.

In a food processor, combine ingredients for a full minute. Scrape the food processor's sides and mix for a further 30 seconds. To serve, put two teaspoons of mixture into each small pastry cup.

78. Carrot Cake

Preparation Time: 5 minutes

Total Time: 25 minutes

Servings: 2

Difficulty Level: Easy

Nutritional Information
Calories: 109 kcal, Protein: 3 g, Carbohydrates: 22 g, Fat: 1 g, Fibers: 3 g

INGREDIENTS

- 1/4 cup flour
- Just over 1/2 tsp cinnamon
- 1/4 tsp baking powder
- 1/8 tsp baking soda
- 1/3 cup of grated, peeled carrots
- 1/8 tsp salt
- 1 1/2 tbsp brown sugar
- Pinch of uncut stevia /1 tbsp of sugar
- 1 tbsp milk of choice
- optional 1/2 tsp ginger or 2 tsp flax meal
- 1 tbsp oil OR more milk of choice
- 1/4 tsp pure vanilla extract

INSTRUCTIONS

This recipe is for 2 servings only. Leftover can be stored in an airtight container in the fridge for 4 days.

In a small bowl, mix dry ingredients (not carrots). Mix all wet ingredients and blend if you have a blender or Magic Bullet. Mix the dry mixture with the wet mixture, and stir. Pour this mixture into a greased little dish. In the case of the microwave, cook for 1 minute 20 seconds. Or cook in the oven at 350 degrees F for around 15 minutes. Let it cool before trying to pop out.

79. Apple Crisp & Oats

Preparation Time: 10 minutes

Total Time: 30 minutes

Servings: 4

Difficulty Level: Easy

Nutritional Information
Calories: 292 kcal, Protein: 7 g, Carbohydrates: 33 g, Fat: 15 g, Fibers: 6 g

---

INGREDIENTS

- 1 tablespoon of coconut oil, melted
- 4 cups of apples peeled plus 1/4-inch-thick sliced pieces; 1 lb.; honey crisp
- 1/4 teaspoon of ground ginger
- 1/2 teaspoon of cinnamon

Crisp Topping

- 1/4 teaspoon of ground ginger
- 1/2 cup of old-fashioned oats
- 1/4 teaspoon of nutmeg
- 1/3 cup of pecans chopped
- 1 tablespoon of maple syrup
- 1/2 teaspoon of cinnamon
- 2 tablespoons of coconut oil

INSTRUCTIONS

This recipe is for 4 servings only. Leftover can be stored in an airtight container in the fridge for 4 days.

Prepare a greased 8x8 baking dish and preheat the oven to 350 degrees F. Peel and slice apples into 1/4-inch-thick pieces. Melt coconut oil. Combine coconut oil, cinnamon, and ginger with apples. Set it aside. Combine a crisp topping. Place apples in the baking dish's base. Apples are covered with a layer of crunchy topping.

Wrap apple crisp with aluminium foil and bake for 20 minutes at 350 degrees F. After twenty minutes, remove the lid and bake for 10 to 20 minutes, until the apples are soft, and the topping turns golden brown.

80. Watermelon Pizza

Preparation Time: 10 minutes

Total Time: 10 minutes

Servings: 4

Difficulty Level: Easy

Nutritional Information
Calories: 93 kcal, Protein: 4 g, Carbohydrates: 17 g, Fat: 1 g, Fibers: 2 g

INGREDIENTS

- 2 large round slices of watermelon about 1 inch thick
- 3/4 cup of Low fat or fat-free plain Greek yogurt
- 1 teaspoon honey
- 1 tsp vanilla extra
- 1 cup fresh strawberries, sliced
- 1 cup fresh blackberries, sliced in half (You may use fresh blueberries if blackberries are unavailable. You can also use bananas or raspberries with, or instead, of strawberries)
- A handful of fresh mint leaves, rough chopped, optional

INSTRUCTIONS

This recipe is for 4 servings only. Leftover can be stored in an airtight container in the fridge for 1 day.

Mix well with yogurt, honey, and vanilla in a bowl. Divide yogurt in half, and spread equal amounts on each watermelon round. Decorate each watermelon round with berries and sprinkle with mint leaves if using. Cut each watermelon round into 8 slices and serve.

81. Coconut Macaroons

Preparation Time: 10 minutes

Total Time: 25 minutes

Servings: 18

Difficulty Level: Easy

Nutritional Information
Calories: 146 kcal, Protein: 2 g, Carbohydrates: 21 g, Fat: 6 g, Fibers: 2 g

---

INGREDIENTS

- 5 1/2 cups of unsweetened coconut flakes; 14-ounce bag
- 1 teaspoon of almond extract
- 14 ounces of evaporated skim milk
- 1 teaspoon of vanilla extract
- 2/3 cup of flour
- 1/4 teaspoon of kosher salt

INSTRUCTIONS

This recipe is for 18 servings only. Leftover can be stored in an airtight container in the fridge for 4 days.

In a large dish, combine the extracts with the evaporated skim milk. Mix the coconut flakes, flour, and salt until well combined. Refrigerate for an hour while covered. Preheat the oven to 350 °F. Bake 18 macaroons on parchment paper in a heated oven for fifteen minutes. Using an ice cream scoop.

82. Easy Sugar-free Cheesecake

Preparation Time: 20 minutes

Total Time: 1hr. refrigeration and 20 minutes

Servings: 8

Difficulty Level: Easy

Nutritional Information
Calories: 187 kcal, Protein: 6 g, Carbohydrates: 16 g, Fat: 11 g, Fibers: 2 g

---

INGREDIENTS

- 1 graham cracker prepared crumb crust
- 1 cup of boiling water
- 1 – 4 serving pkg. of strawberry gelatin; sugar-free
- 2 – 8 oz pkg. of cream cheese; fat-free
- 2 teaspoons of vanilla extract
- 1 cup Fat-Free Cool Whip
- Strawberry slices, optional

INSTRUCTIONS

This recipe is for 8 servings only. Leftover can be stored in an airtight container in the fridge for 3-4 days.

Dissolve strawberry gelatin in boiling water. Let it cool until it starts thickening but not set. In a wide bowl, beat vanilla and cream cheese until smooth. Mix in the strawberry gelatin. Add Cool Whip Free and mix well. Pour filling into the crust. Refrigerate overnight. Garnish with strawberry slices.

83. Peach Cobbler

Preparation Time: 10 minutes
Total Time: 50 minutes
Servings: 6
Difficulty Level: Medium

Nutritional Information
Calories: 223 kcal, Protein: 4 g, Carbohydrates: 36 g, Fat: 7 g, Fibers: 1 g

---

INGREDIENTS

- 1/2 cup of flour
- 1/4 cup of unsalted butter
- 1 teaspoon of baking powder
- 2 cups of peeled peaches; (if frozen; thaw & drain juice)
- 1/2 cup of sugar (divided)
- 1/3 cup of low-fat milk
- 1/4 teaspoon of salt
- 1 egg
- 1/2 teaspoon of cinnamon
- 1/4 tsp of vanilla
- 1/4 teaspoon of nutmeg
- ice cream; for serving (optional)
- 1/4 cup of brown sugar

INSTRUCTIONS

This recipe is for 6 servings only. Leftover can be stored in an airtight container in the fridge for 4 days.

The oven should be heated to 350 degrees Fahrenheit. While the oven preheats, place the butter in a glass dish measuring 9 inches and melt it in the oven. Mix flour, 2/3 cup of sugar, baking powder, and salt in a large bowl. Stir milk and egg into the flour mixture to incorporate. Pour mixture over melted butter into a glass dish. - DO NOT STIR

Place peaches in a dish and combine them with 1/3 cup sugar, cinnamon, vanilla, and nutmeg. Stir to mix ingredients. Gently spoon peaches over the batter. DO NOT STIR. On top of the peaches and batter, sprinkle brown sugar.

Bake for 40 to 45 minutes until the batter turns golden brown. Continue with a few mins in the broiler to crisp up the top (keep a careful eye on it so it will not burn). Serve alongside vanilla ice cream while warm.

84. Banana Mousse

Total Time: 10 mins

Yield:4 servings

Preparation Time: 10 minutes

Total Time: 10 minutes

Servings: 4

Difficulty Level: Easy

Nutritional Information
Calories: 84 kcal, Protein: 4 g, Carbohydrates: 14 g, Fat: 1 g, Fibers: 3 g

INGREDIENTS

- 1 tsp of vanilla
- 2 tsp of brown sugar
- 1 medium banana; quarters
- 8 slices of banana (1/4 inch)
- 2 Tbsp of low-fat milk
- 1 Cup of low-fat plain yogurt

INSTRUCTIONS

This recipe is for 4 servings only. Leftover can be stored in an airtight container in the fridge for 4 days.

Combine the vanilla, brown sugar, milk, and banana in a blender. Process at high speed for 15 seconds or until smooth. Pour the mixture into a small mixing dish and stir in the yogurt. Chill. Before serving, spoon into 4 dessert plates and top with two banana slices for each.

85. Cinnamon Banana Bread Muffins

Preparation Time: 5 minutes

Total Time: 25 minutes

Servings: 12 muffins

Difficulty Level: Medium

Nutritional Information
Calories: 163 kcal, Protein: 3 g, Carbohydrates: 22 g, Fat: 7 g, Fibers: 2 g

---

INGREDIENTS

Banana Bread Muffins

- 2 large eggs
- ½ cup of vegetable /canola oil
- 1 teaspoon of vanilla extract
- ⅔ cup of mashed banana; (2 small bananas)
- 1 teaspoon of baking soda
- 1/2 cup of brown sugar
- 1 ⅔ cup of all-purpose flour
- ½ teaspoon of ground cinnamon
- ½ teaspoon of salt

Cinnamon & Sugar Topping

- ¼ cup of granulated sugar
- ½ teaspoon of ground cinnamon
- 3 tablespoons of butter, melted

INSTRUCTIONS

This recipe is for 12 servings only. Leftover can be stored in an airtight container in the fridge for 4 days.

Preheat oven to 375 ° F. Spray just the bottoms of 12 muffin cups in standard size with cooking spray. You may also use liners. Mix the brown sugar, oil, & eggs in a medium bowl using a wire whisk. Whisk in the bananas and vanilla until blended. Stir the flour, salt, baking soda and cinnamon until just mixed. Evenly pour batter into muffin cups. Each muffin tin will be almost filled. Nearly full.

For 17 to 21 minutes, bake it until a tester inserted in the middle of the muffin emerges clean, and the muffins' tops are high and rounded. The muffins' tops should not seem moist since this indicates that they are not entirely baked. Transfer muffins to a wire cooling rack. In a separate bowl, combine the sugar & cinnamon for the cinnamon-sugar topping. In a separate dish, melt the butter. The muffin tops are dipped in melted butter and, afterwards, cinnamon sugar. Serve warm, or even let it cool thoroughly.

86. Mango Pudding

Preparation Time: 10 minutes

Total Time: 10 minutes

Servings: 2

Difficulty Level: Easy

Nutritional Information
Calories: 300 kcal, Protein: 15 g, Carbohydrates: 24 g, Fat: 16 g, Fiber: 11 g

INGREDIENTS

- 1 cup of plain yogurt
- 1 peeled mango; blended.
- 1 teaspoon of fresh mint
- 3 oz chia seeds

INSTRUCTIONS

This recipe is for 2 servings only.

Combine the plain yogurt and chia seeds in the serving glasses. The yogurt is topped with pureed mango and fresh mint.

87. Egg White Waffles

Preparation Time: 20 minutes

Total Time: 20 minutes

Servings: 2

Difficulty Level: Easy

Nutritional Information
Calories: 147 Kcal, Protein: 19 g, Carbohydrates: 11 g, Fat: 3 g, Fiber: 4 g

---

INGREDIENTS

- 1 teaspoon of baking powder
- ¼ cup of coconut flour
- 6 egg whites
- ¼ cup of almond milk (unsweetened)
- Dash of vanilla extract
- 1 tablespoon of applesauce (unsweetened)

INSTRUCTIONS

This recipe is for 2 servings only.

Oil the waffle iron after preheating it. Combine baking powder and flour in a wide mixing bowl. Stir in the remaining ingredients until well-mixed. Cook until golden brown for 3-4 minutes in a preheated waffle iron with half of the mixture; continue for the rest. Serve warm.

88. Sweet Potato Pie

Preparation Time: 10 minutes
Total Time: 1 hr. 20 minutes
Servings: 16
Difficulty Level: Medium

Nutritional Information
Calories: 127 kcal, Protein: 4 g, Carbohydrates: 21 g, Fat: 3 g, Fibers: 4 g

---

INGREDIENTS

For crust

- 1 tbsp of sugar
- 1 Cup of flour
- 3 Tbsp of vegetable oil
- 1/3 Cup of skim milk

For filling

- 1/4 Cup of brown sugar
- 1/4 Cup of white sugar
- 3 large beaten eggs,
- 1/4 tsp of nutmeg
- 1/2 tsp of salt
- 1/4 Cup of evaporated skim milk; canned
- 3 Cup of cooked, mashed sweet potatoes,
- 1 tsp of vanilla extract

INSTRUCTIONS

This recipe is for 16 servings only. Leftover can be stored in an airtight container in the fridge for 4 days.

Preheat the oven to 350 degrees Fahrenheit. To make the crust, combine sugar and flour in a mixing dish. Add milk and oil to the flour mix. Stir with a fork until everything is thoroughly combined. Then, using your hands, roll the pastry into a smooth ball. In short, quick strokes, roll the ball between two 12-inch pieces of waxed paper until the pastry reaches the edge of the paper. Remove the top paper from the crust and invert it into a 9-inch pie dish. To make the filling, Combine salt, nutmeg, sugars, and eggs in a mixing bowl. Pour in the milk and vanilla extract. Stir. Mix in the sweet potatoes well. Fill the pie shell halfway with the mixture. Bake for 60 minutes or until golden brown on top. Allow cooling before cutting into 16 pieces.

Chapter 10
Air Fryer Recipes

Note: If you find any ingredients that trigger your acid reflux, feel free to omit or change that ingredient.

89. Flaxseed Porridge

Preparation Time: 5 minutes

Total Time: 5 minutes

Servings: 6

Difficulty Level: Medium

Nutritional Information
Calories: 330 kcal, Protein: 13 g, Carbohydrates: 42 g, Fat: 12 g, Fiber: 4 g

---

INGREDIENTS

- 2 cups of steel-cut oats
- 1 cup of flax seeds
- 1 tbsp of peanut butter
- 1 tbsp of unsalted butter
- 4 cups of almond milk
- 4 tbsp of honey

INSTRUCTIONS

This recipe is for 6 servings only. Leftover can be stored in an airtight container in the fridge for 2 days.

Preheat an air fryer to 390 degrees F. Combine all ingredients in an ovenproof bowl. Place in an air fryer and cook for 5 minutes. Stir and serve

90. Mushroom goulash

Preparation Time: 20 mins

Total Time: 1 hour 30 mins

Servings: 3

Difficulty Level: Medium

Nutritional Information
Calories: 281 kcal, Protein: 29 g, Carbohydrates: 14 g, Fat: 11 g, Fiber: 4 g

---

INGREDIENTS

- 2 tbsp. of canola oil
- 1 lb. chicken, boneless, skinless, cubed,
- 1 lb. fresh mushrooms: sliced
- 1 tbsp. of thyme, dried
- 1 cup of green peppers; sliced
- 1 tbsp. of basil
- 1/4 cup of water
- 1 tbsp. of marjoram
- 3 cups of zucchini; diced
- 1 tbsp. of oregano

INSTRUCTIONS

This recipe is for 3 servings only. Leftover can be stored in an airtight container in the fridge for 2 days.

Cut the chicken into cubes. Place them in a pan and an air fryer basket, then pour olive oil. Add zucchini, mushrooms, and green pepper. Stir well and add cook for 2 minutes, then add water and seasonings. Close the air fryer and cook the stew for 50 minutes. Set the heat to 340°F and cook for an additional 20 minutes. Remove from the air fryer and transfer into a large dish.

91. Pumpkin Soup

Preparation Time: 5 minutes

Total Time: 35 minutes

Servings: 4

Difficulty Level: Medium

Nutritional Information
Calories: 190 kcal, Protein: 3 g, Carbohydrates: 13 g, Fat: 14 g, Fiber: 2 g

---

INGREDIENTS

- 4 cups chopped fresh pumpkin
- 3 Tbsp olive oil
- 1 tsp sea salt
- 2 cups chopped carrots
- 1 Tbsp dried chopped thyme
- 1 qt chicken broth
- 1/4 cup heavy cream

INSTRUCTIONS

This recipe is for 4 servings only. Leftover can be stored in an airtight container in the fridge for 2 days.

Preheat your air fryer to 400 degrees F and line the tray or baking pan with foil. Place the pumpkin and carrots on the prepared sheet tray. Sprinkle the veggies with salt, thyme, and olive oil. Roast in the air fryer for 20 minutes or until the squash is tender. Add the roasted veggies to a blender or food processor, and add the chicken broth and heavy cream. Puree until smooth. Serve hot.

92. Tuna Veggie Stir-Fry

Preparation Time: 5 minutes

Total Time: 30 minutes

Servings: 4

Difficulty Level: Medium

Nutritional Information
Calories: 184 kcal, Protein: 17 g, Carbohydrates: 11 g, Fat:8 g, Fiber: 2 g

---

INGREDIENTS

- 1 tablespoon olive oil
- 1 red bell pepper, chopped
- 1 cup green beans, cut into 2-inch pieces
- 2 tablespoons low-sodium soy sauce
- 1 tablespoon honey
- ½ pound fresh tuna, cubed

INSTRUCTIONS

This recipe is for 4 servings only. Leftover can be stored in an airtight container in the fridge for 2 days.

In a 6-inch metal bowl, combine the olive oil, red bell pepper, green beans. Cook in the air fryer for 4 to 6 minutes at 380 F, stirring once, until crisp and tender. Add soy sauce, honey, and tuna, and stir. Cook for another 3 to 6 minutes, stirring once until the tuna is cooked as desired. Tuna can be served rare or medium-rare, or you can cook it until well done.

93. Air Fryer Banana Bread

Preparation Time: 10 minutes

Total Time: 40 minutes

Servings: 6

Difficulty Level: Easy

Nutritional Information
Calories: 299 kcal, Protein: 8 g, Carbohydrates: 33 g, Fat: 15 g, Fiber: 4 g

---

INGREDIENTS

- ¼ tsp of salt
- 2 ripe bananas
- ¼ tsp of baking soda
- ¾ cup of all-purpose flour
- ¼ cup of sour cream
- ½ cup of granulated sugar
- ¼ cup of vegetable oil
- ½ tsp of pure vanilla extract
- ½ cup of chopped walnuts
- 1 large egg

INSTRUCTIONS

This recipe is for 6 servings only. Leftover can be stored in an airtight container in the fridge for 4 days.

Combine salt, flour, and baking soda in a large mixing bowl. In another medium bowl, mash the bananas with a fork or a potato masher until completely smooth. Whisk the oil, sugar, vanilla, sour cream, and egg until well combined.

Toss the wet components with the dry ingredients until just well combined. Don't over-mix the ingredients. If desired, gently whisk in walnuts.

Place the batter in an air fryer basket in a nonstick 6- 7" round baking pan. (Alternatively, you may use the square, tall-sided pan with an air fryer or any other air fryer-safe pan of comparable size.)

Bake at 310°F for 33–37 minutes, or until a toothpick inserted in the center of the bread comes out clean. Allow cooling for at least 20 minutes in a baking pan before slicing it.

94. Banana Fritters

Preparation Time: 5 minutes

Total Time: 15 minutes

Servings: 4

Difficulty Level: Medium

Nutritional Information
Calories: 213 kcal, Protein: 4 g, Carbohydrates: 38 g, Fat: 5 g, Fiber: 1 g

---

INGREDIENTS

- 3 tbsp. of corn flour
- 8 bananas
- 3 tbsp. of vegetable oil
- ¾ cup of breadcrumbs
- 1 egg white

INSTRUCTIONS

This recipe is for 4 servings only. Leftover can be stored in an airtight container in the fridge for 2 days.

Preheat an air fryer to 350 degrees Fahrenheit. In a small mixing bowl, combine oil and breadcrumbs. First, coat the bananas with flour, brush them with egg white, and coat them with a breadcrumb mixture. Place them on a parchment-lined baking sheet, and bake for 8 minutes. Enjoy.

95. Carrot brownies

Preparation Time: 5 minutes

Total Time: 35 minutes

Servings: 6

Difficulty Level: Medium

Nutritional Information
Calories: 239 kcal, Protein: 8 g, Carbohydrates: 21 g, Fat: 13 g, Fiber: 2 g

---

INGREDIENTS

- 1 teaspoon almond extract
- 2 eggs, whisked
- ½ cup butter, melted
- 4 tablespoons sugar
- 2 cups almond flour
- ½ cup carrot, peeled and grated

INSTRUCTIONS

This recipe is for 6 servings only. Leftover can be stored in an airtight container in the fridge for 4 days.

In a bowl, combine the eggs with the butter and the other ingredients, whisk, pour this into a pan that fits your air fryer, and cook at 340 degrees F for 25 minutes. Cool down, slice, and serve.

96. Honey-Apricot Granola with Greek Yogurt

Preparation Time: 5 minutes

Total Time: 40 minutes

Servings: 4

Difficulty Level: Medium

Nutritional Information
Calories: 348 kcal, Protein: 20 g, Carbohydrates: 31 g, Fat: 16 g, Fiber: 4 g

---

INGREDIENTS

- 1 cup rolled oats
- ¼ cup dried apricots, diced
- ¼ cup almond slivers
- ¼ cup walnuts, chopped
- ¼ cup pumpkin seeds
- ¼ cup hemp hearts
- ¼ to ⅓ cup raw honey, plus more for drizzling
- 1 tablespoon olive oil
- 1 teaspoon ground cinnamon
- ¼ teaspoon ground nutmeg
- ¼ teaspoon salt
- 3 cups nonfat plain Greek yoghurt

INSTRUCTIONS

This recipe is for 4 servings only. Leftover can be stored in an airtight container in the fridge for 1 day.

Preheat the air fryer to 260°F. Line the air fryer basket with parchment paper. In a large bowl, combine the oats, apricots, almonds, walnuts, pumpkin seeds, hemp hearts, honey, olive oil, cinnamon, nutmeg, and salt, mixing honey, oil, and spices are well distributed. Pour the mixture onto the parchment paper and spread it into an even layer. Bake for 10 minutes, shake or stir and spread out into an even layer. Continue baking for 10 minutes more, then repeat the process of shaking or stirring the mixture. Bake for an additional 10 minutes before removing it from the air fryer. Allow the granola to cool completely, and pour it into an airtight container for storage. For each serving, top ½ cup Greek yoghurt with ⅓ cup granola and a drizzle of honey, if needed.

97. Zucchini lasagna

Preparation Time: 5 minutes

Total Time: 30 minutes

Servings: 2

Difficulty Level: Easy

Nutritional Information
Calories: 319 kcal, Protein: 14 g, Carbohydrates: 32 g, Fat: 15 g, Fiber: 3 g

---

INGREDIENTS

- Generous pinch of salt
- 2 lasagna noodles
- ¼ cup of tofu ricotta
- ½ cup of bechamel sauce
- 1 handful of fresh basil leaves; chopped; about ¼ cup and more for garnish
- 3 Tablespoons of shredded zucchini
- 1 handful of baby spinach leaves; chopped; about ¼ cup

INSTRUCTIONS

This recipe is for 2 servings only. Leftover can be stored in an airtight container in the fridge for 2 days.

Straight down from the middle, cut 2 lasagna noodles in half. You'll end up with four 5-inch-long noodles after breaking them.

Add a generous amount of salt in water in a soup pot and bring it to a boil. Follow the package instructions for boiling the noodles in this water. (It will take 8-10 minutes.) Drain the noodles and set them aside. Then place them on a clean kitchen towel to dry them completely.

Take a 5.75-inch small loaf pan. Add 2 Tablespoons of bechamel sauce to line the bottom of a loaf pan. Then place one 5-inch noodle on top. About a Tablespoon of tofu ricotta, a pinch of chopped spinach, a pinch of chopped basil, and a pinch of shredded zucchini go on top of the noodle. Distribute the ingredients equally on the noodles.

Add another noodle now. Repeat the layering step. Then place another noodle and repeat it. Finally, add the last noodle and add a few more tbsp. Of sauce, sprinkle tofu ricotta on top, ensuring the noodles are well covered.

Wrap aluminium foil around the loaf pan. In the air fryer, place the loaf pan. Air fries the lasagna for 10 minutes at 400 degrees F. Then, remove the loaf pan and the aluminium foil from the fryer. Air fry it for 3 to 5 minutes more or until the top of the lasagna has a great color and crispiness. Wait 2-3 minutes to help remove the lasagna easily when cooled, and serve it.

98. Sweet Potato Ginger Salad

Preparation Time: 5 minutes

Total Time: 25 minutes

Servings: 2

Difficulty Level: Medium

Nutritional Information
Calories: 259 kcal, Protein: 3 g, Carbohydrates: 28 g, Fat:15 g, Fiber: 3 g

INGREDIENTS

- 2 sweet potatoes, peeled and cut into wedges
- Salt to taste
- 2 tablespoons avocado oil
- ¼ teaspoon coriander, ground
- 2 tsp low-fat mayonnaise
- ½ teaspoon cumin, ground
- A pinch of ginger powder
- A pinch of cinnamon powder

Instruction:

This recipe is for 2 servings only.

Mix the sweet potato wedges in your air fryer's basket with salt, coriander and oil; toss well. Cook at 370 degrees F for 20 minutes, flipping them once. Transfer the potatoes to a bowl, and add the mayonnaise, cumin, ginger, and cinnamon. Toss and serve as a side salad.

Chapter 11
Acid Reflux Teas

Note: If you find any ingredients that trigger your acid reflux, feel free to omit or change that ingredient.

99. Chamomile Tea

Preparation Time: 5 minutes

Total Time: 5 minutes

Servings: 2

Difficulty Level: Easy

Nutritional Information
Calories: 20 kcal, Protein: 0 g, Carbohydrates: 5 g, Fat: 0 g, Fiber: 0 g

---

INGREDIENTS

- 2 cups Water
- 1 tbsp honey
- 3 teaspoons Dried Chamomile

INSTRUCTIONS

This recipe is for 2 servings only.

Bring water to a boil in a pot over high heat. As soon as the water begins to boil, turn off the heat and add dried Chamomile. Keep the lid on for one minute. Pour the chamomile tea through a strainer into the teacups, stir it up, and serve.

100. Fennel Tea

Preparation Time: 5 minutes

Total Time: 15 minutes

Servings: 2

Difficulty Level: Easy

Nutritional Information
Calories: 12 kcal, Protein: 0 g, Carbohydrates: 3 g, Fat: 0 g, Fiber: 0 g

INGREDIENTS

- 1 tablespoon of crushed fennel seeds
- 1/2 teaspoon of honey
- 1 1/2 cups of water
- 3 mint leaves
- 1/4 inch of lightly crushed ginger

INSTRUCTIONS

This recipe is for 2 servings only.

Combine all ingredients and let it boil. Covered for at least 10 minutes. Serve hot.

101. Ginger Tea

Preparation Time: 10 minutes

Total Time: 5 minutes

Servings: 2

Difficulty Level: Easy

Nutritional Information
Calories: 20 kcal, Protein: 0 g, Carbohydrates: 5 g, Fat: 0 g, Fiber: 0 g

---

INGREDIENTS

- 3 tablespoons grated Gingerroot
- 1 tbsp honey
- 3 cups Boiling water

INSTRUCTIONS

This recipe is for 2 servings only.

Combine all ingredients and allow to boil. Covered for at least 10 minutes. Serve hot.

102. Licorice Root Tea

Preparation Time: 5 minutes
Total Time: 10 minutes
Servings: 2
Difficulty Level: Easy

Nutritional Information
Calories: 28 kcal, Protein: 1 g, Carbohydrates: 6 g, Fat: 0 g, Fiber: 0 g

INGREDIENTS

- honey, to taste
- 5 cups of water
- 1 oz dried licorice root; roughly chopped, if using fresh

INSTRUCTIONS

This recipe is for 2 servings only.

Combine all ingredients and allow to boil. Covered for at least 10 minutes. Serve hot.

103. Slippery Elm Tea

Preparation Time: 5 minutes

Total Time: 5 minutes

Servings: 2

Difficulty Level: Easy

Nutritional Information
Calories: 34 kcal, Protein: 1 g, Carbohydrates: 7 g, Fat: 1 g, Fiber: 0 g

---

INGREDIENTS

- 1 cup of boiling water
- 1 tbsp. of slippery elm bark (powdered)
- 1 tbsp of organic blackstrap molasses; unsulfured or other sweeteners
- 1 dash of cinnamon / nutmeg; for added flavor; if desired
- 2-3 oz of light coconut milk /other milk

INSTRUCTIONS

This recipe is for 2 servings only.

Pour boiling water into a cup, add powdered bark, and mix well. Add any other ingredients you like, and enjoy.

Conclusion

Heartburn, or a burning feeling in the chest, is a common symptom of acid reflux or GERD, especially after eating and at night. A persistent cough or trouble swallowing are some acid reflux symptoms.

Diet has a strong significant link with GERD. Along with medicine, lifestyle, dietary, and integrative changes might be beneficial. Acid reflux symptoms may be brought on or made worse by certain meals and beverages. If you're one of the millions of individuals with acid reflux or GERD, you know how unpleasant or painful it is, and certain meals might exacerbate your symptoms. If you often get heartburn or acid reflux, you should keep a two-week food diary to record everything you eat. To understand better which meals may aggravate your symptoms, keep track of the days you get acid reflux.

Acid reflux discomfort may be lessened by reducing the consumption of items known to cause GERD, such as coffee, chocolate, fatty foods, alcohol, red sauces, and carbonated drinks. The symptoms of GERD may also be lessened by eating smaller meal amounts during the day and avoiding lying down for at least 2 or 3 hours after a meal. Along with diet, smoking and being overweight are major causes of acid reflux. Surgery may tighten a lower oesophagal sphincter if none of these methods works.

The right medical care should stop GERD from impairing a person's quality of life. However, a doctor must always be consulted before making any alterations to a treatment regimen.

This book is helpful if you are sick of coping with the terrible GERD & acid reflux symptoms or are just looking for solutions to handle the digestive ailment better. Recipes in this book are designed specifically for patients suffering from GERD.

Meal Plan

A meal plan provides support when you adjust your diet. You may continue eating healthily every day since the recipes are a part of the meal plan. These meal plans may help you stay on schedule, save money, prepare quickly, save time, and minimize waste. Here is a 28-days meal plan to help you manage acid reflux.

DAY 1
- **Breakfast:** Sweet Potato Protein Hash
- **Lunch:** Chicken Salad Sandwich
- **Snack:** Banana-Apple Smoothie
- **Dinner:** Chicken Stir Fry

DAY 2
- **Breakfast:** Oatmeal Yogurt Bowl
- **Lunch:** Zucchini Pasta with Ground Turkey and Fresh Peaches
- **Snack:** Chamomile tea
- **Dinner:** Balsamic Chicken

DAY 3
- **Breakfast:** Chia Pudding
- **Lunch:** Shrimp Soup
- **Snack:** Ginger tea
- **Dinner:** Baked Chicken Meatballs

DAY 4
- **Breakfast:** Guava Smoothie
- **Lunch:** Chicken with Green Vegetables
- **Dinner:** Tomato Sauce-Free Lasagna
- **Dessert:** Carrot Cake

DAY 5
- **Breakfast:** Zucchini Bread
- **Lunch:** Chickpea and Garden Pea Stew
- **Snack:** Elm tea
- **Dinner:** Banh mi bowls & sticky tofu

DAY 6
- **Breakfast:** Avocado Berry Breakfast
- **Lunch:** Vegan Tacos
- **Dinner:** Crispy Broiled Haddock with Broccolini
- **Dessert:** Sweet potato pie

DAY 7
- **Breakfast:** French Toast
- **Lunch:** Carrot Ginger Soup
- **Snack:** Yogurt cereal bowl
- **Dinner:** Maple BBQ Salmon

DAY 8
- **Breakfast:** Beet & Berries Smoothie Bowl
- **Lunch:** Chicken Salad
- **Dinner:** Sweet Potato Noodles
- **Dessert:** Apple cake

DAY 9
- **Breakfast:** Zucchini Fritters
- **Lunch:** Shredded Chicken and Berry Salad
- **Snack:** Ginger tea
- **Dinner:** Root Vegetables and Apricot Chicken Thighs

DAY 10
- **Breakfast**: Oatmeal Breakfast Cookies
- **Lunch:** Chicken Salad Sandwich
- **Dinner:** Summer Squash Pasta
- **Dessert:** Pumpkin cheesecake bites

DAY 11
- **Breakfast:** French Toast
- **Lunch:** Vegan Tacos
- **Snack:** Fennel tea
- **Dinner:** Chicken Stir Fry

DAY 12
- **Breakfast:** Pureed Banana Oats
- **Lunch:** Creamy Leek and Salmon Soup
- **Snack:** Licorice Root Tea
- **Dinner:** Bakes Chicken Meatballs

DAY 13
- **Breakfast:** Avocado Berry Breakfast
- **Lunch:** Vegan Tacos
- **Dinner:** Crispy Broiled Haddock with Broccolini
- **Dessert:** Apple crisp & oats

DAY 14
- **Breakfast:** California Scrambles Eggs and Avocado
- **Lunch:** Turmeric Coconut Cauliflower Bowls
- **Snack:** Fennel tea
- **Dinner:** Chicken with Green Vegetables

DAY 15
- **Breakfast:** Strawberry Banana Smoothie
- **Lunch:** Honey Mustard Chicken & Potato
- **Snack:** Ginger tea
- **Dinner:** Carrot Ginger Soup

DAY 16
- **Breakfast:** Kale and Sweet Potato Baked Frittata Cups
- **Lunch:** Balsamic Chicken
- **Dinner:** Vegan Tacos
- **Dessert:** watermelon pizza

DAY 17
- **Breakfast:** Sweet Potato Protein Hash
- **Lunch:** Chicken Salad Sandwich
- **Snack:** Fennel tea
- **Dinner:** Chicken Stir Fry

DAY 18
- **Breakfast:** Guava Smoothie
- **Lunch:** Chicken with Green Vegetables
- **Dinner:** Tomato Sauce-Free Lasagna
- **Dessert:** Apple crisp & oats

DAY 19
- **Breakfast:** Chia Pudding
- **Lunch:** Shrimp Soup
- **Snack:** Banana-Apple Smoothie
- **Dinner:** Baked Chicken Meatballs

DAY 20
- **Breakfast:** Oatmeal Yogurt Bowl
- **Lunch:** Zucchini Pasta with Ground Turkey and Fresh Peaches
- **Dinner:** Balsamic Chicken

DAY 21
- **Breakfast:** Avocado Berry Breakfast
- **Lunch:** Vegan Tacos
- **Snack:** Fennel tea
- **Dinner:** Crispy Broiled Haddock with Broccolini

DAY 22
- **Breakfast:** Beet & Berries Smoothie Bowl
- **Lunch:** Chicken Salad
- **Dinner:** Sweet Potato Noodles
- **Dessert:** Apple crisp & oats

DAY 23
- **Breakfast:** California Scrambles Eggs and Avocado
- **Lunch:** Turmeric Coconut Cauliflower Bowls
- **Dinner:** chicken with green vegetables
- **Dessert:** Watermelon pizza

DAY 24
- **Breakfast**: Oatmeal Breakfast Cookies
- **Lunch:** Shrimp Soup
- **Snack:** Banana-Apple Smoothie
- **Dinner:** Summer Squash Pasta

DAY 25
- **Breakfast:** Pureed Banana Oats
- **Lunch:** Creamy Leek and Salmon Soup
- **Dinner:** Baked Chicken Meatballs
- **Dessert:** Carrot Cake

DAY 26
- **Breakfast:** Sweet Potato Protein Hash
- **Lunch:** Chicken Salad Sandwich
- **Snack:** Fennel tea
- **Dinner:** Chicken Stir Fry

DAY 27
- **Breakfast:** French Toast
- **Lunch:** Carrot Ginger Soup
- **Dinner:** Maple BBQ Salmon
- **Dessert:** Carrot Cake

DAY 28
- **Breakfast:** Oatmeal Yogurt Bowl
- **Lunch:** Zucchini Pasta with Ground Turkey and Fresh Peaches
- **Snack:** Banana-Apple Smoothie
- **Dinner:** Balsamic Chicken

Conversion Tables

There are two widely employed measuring schemes in nutrition: Metric and US Customary.

DRY MEASURE EQUIVALENT			
3 teaspoons	1/2 ounce	1 tablespoon	14.3 grams
2 tablespoons	1 ounce	1/8 cup	28.3 grams
4 tablespoons	2 ounces	1/4 cup	56.7 grams
5 1/3 tablespoons	2.6 ounces	1/3 cup	75.6 grams
8 tablespoons	4 ounces	1/2 cup	113.4 grams
12 tablespoons	6 ounces	3/4 cup	.375 pound
32 tablespoons	16 ounces	2 cups	1 pound

WEIGHT (MASS)	
Metric (grams)	US contemporary (ounces)
14 grams	1/2 ounce
28 grams	1 ounce
85 grams	3 ounces
100 grams	3.53 ounces
113 grams	4 ounces
227 grams	8 ounces
340 grams	12 ounces
454 grams	16 ounces or 1 pound

VOLUME (LIQUID)	
Metric	US Customary
.6 ml	1/8 tsp
1.2 ml	1/4 tsp
2.5 ml	1/2 tsp
3.7 ml	3/4 tsp
5 ml	1 tsp
15 ml	1 tbsp
30 ml	2 tbsp
59 ml	2 fluid ounces or1/4 cup
118 ml	1/2 cup
177 ml	3/4 cup
237 ml	1 cup or 8 fluid ounces
1.9 liters	8 cups or 1/2 gallon

OVEN TEMPERATURES	
Metric	US contemporary
121° C	250° F
149° C	300° F
177° C	350° F
204° C	400° F
232° C	450° F

Made in the USA
Middletown, DE
12 October 2023

40674629R00075